Daughter
OUTLAW

BOOK 1: THE BRUTALITY OF LOVE

STAR BESIO

Cover Featuring MaKenzie Jo

ISBN 978-1-63961-454-7 (paperback)
ISBN 978-1-63961-455-4 (digital)

Christian Faith Publishing, Inc.
832 Park Avenue
Meadville, PA 16335
www.christianfaithpublishing.com

Printed in the United States of America

Acknowledgments

I would like to say thank you!

To God for *all* the lessons that I was taught throughout this life.

To my Grandma Barbara for encouraging me to write since I can remember.

To Jeremy Sharp, without you, I would have been lost.

To my brother, Eddie Haskins, for understanding me when I did not.

To *all* of my parents and all the parents who do the *best* they can with what they have.

To *all* of my children and the ones that call me "Aunt" something or another, you are my heart.

To *all* of my blood and nonblood brothers and sisters who have supported all of my good and bad decisions and are still here with me.

To *all* of my fallen friends and loved ones that are not here with me today, and for the impact you all have made.

To Brandon Wilson, even death cannot separate.

And last but not the least, to *all* my readers. You make this all worth the struggle to finish the race.

Though this book is based on a true story, any likeness in name, character, or event is purely coincidental and does not reflect fact, only the perception and imagination of a traumatized child.

Chapter 1

They call me Daughter. I am not the only girl, but it seemed fitting enough at the time, I guess. Daddy was on the run and said names are just made for people who want to be found. He gave me a new last name too. Said I was the first with our true last name, but that I had better live up to it or I would be banned from the family for life. Daughter Outlaw. That's me.

I spent the first years of my life watching and learning. Daddy said he thought something was wrong with me because I barely spoke a word until I was six. Only a few times can I recall that silence being out of fear. I worshiped the ground he walked on. He was a god to me. The police called him Satan, but the name made no difference to me. He was my hero. He taught me how to push my own limits and break through mental and physical barriers that would kill weaker adults. We ran drills on what to say to cops, how to talk in code, how to manipulate people, how to panhandle, and how to read folks based on their body language, facial expressions, speech, clothes, accessories, accents, and more. He taught us how to swim, hike, hunt, fish, make a fire, chop wood, jump trains, and make an entire campground with little or nothing. We learned about the wildlife, scorpions to mosquitoes. The entire family consisted five kids and two adults and, at one point in time, an unkin' uncle and his dog.

In the cities, we would sneak in to let Daddy pull a job, then score some dope. Normally, we could stay a night or two in one of some old outlaws' houses, just long enough to shower and wish we did not have to leave. Daddy taught me how to cook too and how to lie and defend my life against a full-grown man. He was big on loyalty and demanded respect. He did not stand more than five feet, seven inches tall or weigh more than 145 pounds, but not a single man did not fear him. They all did whatever he said, like soldiers waiting for command.

When he was not worried about the law, we would have all kinds of fun and adventures. He knew of the most beautiful and amazing places on earth—from the Redwood Forest, Great Salt Lakes, clear mountain streams, places to pick wild fresh fruit, to the tops of the Cascades, or boardwalks on the ocean. When I grew up, we did not have to wear a bathing suit. Everyone swam naked or in their underwear. It was neat to be able to feel so free. On occasion, it sucks so bad you wanted to die (from hunger, walking, or getting a real ass-whooping), but you did not have permission to die from Daddy, so you just kept going.

You had to learn how to leave things behind that you loved, such as people, dogs, toys, blankets. Daddy said there is nothing that cannot be replaced as fast as it was lost except for the group of us—Daddy, my stepmom, stepbrother, older sister, little brother, baby sister, and Uncle. But we eventually parted ways with him too.

It seemed that we always got a vehicle somehow. We were always going somewhere or had a new plan. Though we never stayed long enough before it was time to go. Rest stops and forests were the number-one spots we lived. There was money to be made at rest stops back then. Panhandling or selling crafts. I do not even know if you can vend without a permit at a rest stop now, and as far as I know panhandling is not allowed either. Not the way we would do it anyway. The forest was for longer stays and very necessary after a trip to a city. Daddy also said one day that we would rob a bank together. I was being groomed as his righthand man. It was a hard way to live, but on the upside, we had each other and we got to see the nation.

He was a kid at heart and was always goofing around. He showed us cool-kid stuff like how to eat worms, how to roll joints, or how to chug a mug of beer. My brother was always asked how he was to kiss a girl. At two years old, he would French kiss the air and roll his tongue around his lips. But not long after he was trying to kiss his sisters and every girl like that. I figure that was what made it so funny.

He fed us pizza, a lot. Even the baby. If you had teeth, you got a whole slice on your own. If you did not, you got mostly toppings. But we all got beer and quarters for the arcade. We drank forty proof NyQuil to go to bed or had a puff off one of the joints. We thought it was like a rite of passage. Daddy thought it was a great babysitting tactic and hilarious to watch us fall all over or crawl everywhere.

Sometimes I would wake up and not know where I was. Not because I could not remember, but because he had to emergency-relocate us in the middle of the night. I paid a lot of attention to him. Reading him helped me know what he expected of me or when something was wrong. He used us as lookouts for a lot of things. Though, when they came for him, there was not really a way to stop it. We were also told to think for ourselves. He let us do whatever we wanted unless it would bring negative consequences on him. It made us feel respected and like we were equal.

We were all mean as hell and bred for battle. We would dish out just as much ass-whooping as the one we could take from Daddy. The family could fight amongst ourselves, but you would get stabbed by the toddler if you tried messing with any one of us. Daddy liked to let us pick each other's punishment. All the choices were bad, but each kid did not like one more than the other. If we were mad at one another, then we would choose that one for them. If we were trying to protect each other, the choice would be the one that bothered them the least.

Us kids got together under the watch of my older sister. We would take our cues from her. She was really like our mom. Though she was only a year older than me, three years older than the boys, and seven years older than the baby. Candy Wine is the name the gypsies we ran with gave her. Bubba just called her Doe-Doe. My stepbrother they called Hellion, and the youngest was Baby Girl. My stepmother we called Wicked Witch Bitch, but not to her face. It was Mom. Of course, we all called him Daddy. On occasion, it was the Boogeyman.

Somehow, I do not believe Outlaw was our true last name, but that does not mean it was not in our damn blood. He bred and beat the fear right out of us. He lit a fire full of passion and adventure inside our hearts and crammed common sense, book, and street knowledge down our throats with pitched forks. We were brainwashed into his perfect little minions. We were sponges ready to soak it all up; computers to be programmed. I wanted it. I wanted to make him proud. Though his wrath was hell on earth, his love was unconditional.

He was only in his early twenties, had five kids, a seventh-grade education, and he and his wife were strung out on drugs. They could have sent us away at any time, gave us to CPS, or shipped us to a relative. No, instead, they made a way. So what if it was strong armed robbery and prostitution? Thing is, I thought everyone lived like we did. I did not grasp the concept of having a home. Nor did I know that people kept jobs that they went to everyday or even their whole lives. I knew that when we needed money, we got it. A car, we got it. A place to sleep in, we got it. Drugs, we got them. Christmas, it happened. Birthdays, they happened. Hungry, we ate. Only once do I remember going six days without food. But we walked so long across the entire state of California down an empty highway that we had to stop and make a bullshit camp. No forest, no supplies, nothing but the clothes on our backs. By the first exit in the city, I expected to eat.

Daddy was a little scary-looking to good Samaritans though, so it took a few exits. When we did eat, we ate like kings. That meal also came with a ride and a wad of cash—three birds with one stone.

Daddy said, "A kid can be a goldmine or your worst nightmares come true. People do things to kids." He always warned, "Strangers hurt and steal children. Even cops." I did not know that it was people you loved and trusted as well back then. Or maybe, it was just that I did not love and trust anyone till I was older, except for Daddy, and made to believe that people are good. I am not sure that lines up with the Bible, though. I believe it states that we are all born into sin. It is in our blood. Eating from that tree is what poisoned our blood. We are cursed by the wrath of God for a life of sin. So I guess Daddy was right. We were born outlaws. All of us. Some of us were taught to embrace it, and others were told to hide or deny it. You cannot fool me, though. I can see the lies in all your hearts and lives. Only because I have been watching it my whole entire life.

Chapter 2

You see, Mama, well, she was a different story. You would have never known by the life she led when I met her that she would have ever been with the likes of a man like Daddy. I would have bet my whole damn life on it. She is that good! Hell, I had bet my whole heart and future on the fact that she was not using me to find out where Daddy was, but the bruises on my face and the knots on my head served as reminders of just how wrong I was. Sad thing is that she honestly believed with all her being that Daddy was the devil, that there was not a good or decent thing in that man, only pure evil. But knowing that, she still went on and put me in that position. I guess I was just worth sacrificing if she had a chance. I cannot say whether she really thought it out or not. I know that desperate people do irrational things, but they say, "The road to hell was paved with good intentions."

I met her when I was six years old. She got tired of sending Daddy money for kids she never got the opportunity to see and did not believe that he even still had any of us. Daddy refused to send us all. He told me that she would never send us back. Instead, he decided to send me with a message. That message was to send me back or never see the others again. Simple enough, I thought.

We had never really talked about Mama much. I vaguely remembered what she looked like from a picture I saw at Grandpa's house. I was supposed to be excited. I thought it was pretty rad that Daddy picked me and that I was going to fly on an airplane all by myself. On top of that, Daddy and I got to go on an adventure by ourselves. As for excited about Mama, well, I would have to practice that on the plane to Texas.

We hitchhiked to Grandma's house from Bakersfield.

He decided to invite himself to Mama's parents' house until I returned. He said it was a backup plan. "In case she tries anything stupid." He seemed overly confident that I was coming back, though, so I trusted his confidence enough to hug him goodbye without a tear in my eyes.

The world she lived in and the one I had just walked out of were so far from one another that the only way I knew how to be was to do just the opposite of what Daddy would want. I stayed quiet and just watched as usual. I was taking in my surroundings and trying to analyze it all. It was like being in a picture show, one like my uncle used to play for us at the drive-in theater he worked at for a while. Everyone seemed to expect you to act like they did or to even know what that would be.

There were all new clothes and shoes I was to wear. Girl stuff! A porcelain doll, but I could not play with her because she might break, which did not make much sense. Hell, we threw bottles at each other and played on construction sites. Maybe she did not have those nearby. We went to the zoo. We actually paid to ride a train! When I expressed how "Bitchin'!" I thought the animals were in the middle of the crowd, it seemed to embarrass her tremendously.

She made meals regularly and in the kitchen! We all sat at a table to eat. I had a bed in my own room. All by myself. In the *dark*! I had to take a bath and brush my teeth before bed. Every night.

I had to ask permission to go outside and could not go unless someone was there to watch me. Watch me do what? It made me wonder if she knew we were smoking cigarettes behind Daddy's back when they left us butts in the ashtray. No matter, she smoked too, so I doubt if she would notice if I did.

Still, I had to have her or her boyfriend with me all the time. Even in the tub! First time I took a bath, she tried to wash my body for me. Can you believe that? Daddy said to be nice and just do as she asked because it would benefit us all when it was over. So I just smiled and asked politely, "Is it okay if I wash my own body?" I think that made her uncomfortable, but better her than me.

She seemed nice but did not appear to know what to do with me. Instead, she just made a whole bunch of plans to do all kinds of stuff I think she believed I had never done before. I would like to commend myself for my award-winning acting now. Deep down, though, I could see that she really wanted me to like her. It kind of seemed like she was attempting to compete for my love (between her and Daddy). I did like her, well-enough. She was nice, not very physically affectionate but compensated by always buying me cool stuff or anything, really. Made me wonder if she had let me have a pack of smokes. Honestly, I knew better. I think I just wanted to see what she would say. I never could quite bring myself to let her see me in *that way*. There was an unsaid dislike for Daddy's *kind* that hung in the air like stale barroom smoke. No one ever said anything, but it was obvious to me. I do not think she ever really thought to herself that *that kind* may have included me.

By the end of the visit, I was glad to be headed back, but I was sad. Because, I guess, I did love her. Not more than Daddy, but more than the Wicked Witch Bitch, for sure. Bitch burned me with cigarettes when Daddy was not around.

On the day I was to return, she asked me if I knew how to use a telephone. She walked me through a series of instructions on how to make a collect call. Then she jotted her number down on the back of a Garbage Pail kid sticker and said it was *our little secret* when we were done. All I could think was, "Oh god, I really wish she hadn't done that to me." She knew Daddy would be mad, but she led me to believe that it was just because he did not want me to love her more than him. She led me to believe that it was okay to keep a secret from Daddy. Daddy said secrets were like lies and only to be kept from the police.

Sissy said that we had to protect ourselves and sometimes secrets did that, so it was up to each of us to decide what we kept to ourselves. Like the things I did with the older boys, I was allowed to keep those things to myself. None of us kids told each other's business. We left that up to each other to decide what anyone else would or could be told. There was no tricking us out of it either. We knew better. So I guess Mama's secret really was not all that bad.

Her last few words were to call her from payphones wherever we went and that she loved me and wished that she could keep me with her "always". I told her that I loved her too and meant it when I promised to do as she asked. "Just between us." Somewhere, deep down, I felt that gut-wrenching notion that somehow I would regret it, but Daddy said that we were supposed to keep our word. "Sometimes a man's word is all he may have to work with one day, and it would be good if it were of value when that day came."

I thought I would be more enthusiastic to see Daddy, but I was tired from the entire week and the flight home. Grandma gave us until the next morning before we had to go. Thank God because I do not think I could have made it hitchhiking after the day I had. My thoughts raced, my emotions were high, and I was very confused. Was it wrong to be loyal to both of your parents? What if they hated one another? Did I think Daddy really cared if I loved Mama? I do not think that Daddy ever thought that I would love Mama. I think Mama thought that I remembered who she was. People sure do expect a whole lot from each other. That I do know. It sure does wear a kid out trying to fulfill all those expectations. I wonder if they ever feel the same way. Mama might. Daddy does not care what anyone else expects of him. He will do and say whatever he wants. Always has. Why change now? I wish I could feel that way. I sure bet that it would make things easier.

The first couple calls from the local payphone at the cheap hotel we were living at in Bakersfield felt more like betrayal than love. I missed her, so it became a little easier after a while. At the end of each call, she would ask me weird questions, though. Questions such as if I could read the street signs for her or to read to her the address on the payphone that was usually rubbed off at the bottom. I did my best to appease her, but she kept pushing at it so hard that it made me want to stop calling, but I did not want to hurt her feelings.

I look back and imagine how my life would have been if I had just left her alone. As a child, you just want to be loved. All the shit I went through or sucked up was for *love*! Mama was the first to ruin that for me. Daddy found that phone number written in pencil on the back of that card. He did not have to ask whose it was because he already knew. We were packed and ready to move within five minutes. Everyone waited the last five minutes in the car while Daddy took the time to bounce my head off everything in that hotel room. Afterward, he gave me a towel and exactly one more minute to pull my shit together and walk out with some sort of dignity. That is *not* the feeling I would describe as I held my head high and strutted out the hotel door.

The only emotions that were running through me were *hate* and *anger*! No. Let me back up. Betrayal! Where the hell was she? Halfway across the country. Safe and sound. It was not until the next day that I fully understood the depths of her intentions.

When the cops got Daddy, everything went in slow motion. It did not seem real. We had been in this position before, but, for some reason, I just knew that he would not be coming back. I do not know how; I just did. Maybe I read it on his face. I believe it was in the tears. You know, the ones that he never cried. When he threw up his hands and signed "I love you," it tore a hole in my heart so deep that there was no more room left for love. And Mama, *I hated that bitch*! I was mad at myself more than anything. She played me, and I knew it. I just wanted to believe it was not true because I wanted a mother. So I lied to myself. I went against my gut. Against all I was bred to be aware of, and I trusted her. I saw her world and believed that people were good. She was just a pretender. After all, she used to be just like *Daddy*!

Chapter 3

"**A**sh'ala Ratha E'lune. Wrapped around your sparkling soul is the cursed beauty of a gypsy's toll. Tinker. Tinker. Oh, how you shine, whilst you steal this life o'mine. Ash'ala Ratha E'lune." It would begin as a whisper. The leaves in the forest would rustle, and the campfire would crackle. Then the acoustics from a softly strummed guitar would lull in the background of the darkness. They would all bleed out from their campers or the forest slowly. One by one. You could tell it was a gypsy and not an animal by the *tink* they made when they walked. Decked down from head to toe with rings on their fingers and what seemed like shackles on their souls. Chanting and smirking with half-cocked attitudes as well as minds. Half-mad they all appeared, but I was mesmerized by the sound and the pop of the flames. The moon and the night appeared to chime in regularly. Louder and louder, it would get. Almost as if they were calling a presence I was unaware even existed.

I sat eagerly on a boulder about ten feet from the fire with the forest at my back and the prairie laid before me. The dark-haired beauty with jewelry slung across her body and tacked through her skin grabbed my hand, laid it in hers, and placed her other over the top of it. She had lips that took up the entire bottom half of her face. Her teeth were very white against her dark red lipstick. Bandanna in her hair that matched. Smiling wide, she leaned into my ear. "Ash'ala Ratha E'lune," she murmured.

Reaching down she picked up a dark-brown glass jug with a single hoop at the top near the mouth of it and took a long swig.

Bloodred liquid dripped lightly from the bottom of her lip as she pulled it away. I gazed at her in awe. Leaning forward, she poured the contents of the jug onto my left ear. As she did, she wiped her mouth with the sleeve of the opposite arm. "What's that?" snuck out of my mouth without permission. She leaned her head back and roared with laughter. Handing me the jug, she said, "Go on. 'Tis a rite of passage, I suppose. We call it candied brandy wine." Then I swallowed.

It tasted absolutely amazing. Something warm and delicious tickled my belly, and I knew I would be drunk by the time she began. I braced myself while she pierced the needle on the end of the cork straight through my ear. Feeling and hearing a small pop, I knew it was over. All that remained was the insertion of the bloodred ruby into the small incision after. The barefoot enchantress flipped her hair to throw down another swallow, helped me to my feet, and I skipped off to the beat of the music.

Daddy loved to know how much pain we could handle without crying. I never understood that until I was older. Once I did, I could see its value. There is not much physically that has been able to cause me pain that I would consider remarkable or noteworthy. Any more than I can recall. Daddy snatched me up in his arms and said, "Now, for your sister!" Sissy sure did not have any problems with her piercing, either. Though, I did enjoy watching the clan of wild gypsies jig to the tune of a song written about their candied brandy wine. That was when the horde decided to grant her the nickname Candy Wine. Mine was some sort of Elvin-tongued nickname, E'lune. Ash'ala Ratha E'lune referred to the most beautiful of stars. I never quite thought of myself as beautiful, especially not as beautiful or amazing as the stars in the heavens.

It used to make me question people's intentions with me. You know? Because flattery is a tactic of charm and deceit. It is used in many of my own styles of manipulation that Daddy taught me. It left me wondering if all those stories of gypsies being thieves was true. Maybe. I do know this: those gypsies never stole from us. Could have been Daddy that scared them, but somehow, something told me it was just out of mutual respect.

Later Daddy explained that outlaws have a *code*. We are to live by that code. Then he proceeded to explain a list of values to me, things he felt I should know about unsaid and unwritten rules. "Honor amongst thieves" he called it. I sat in his arms on a log by the fire, mesmerized as he went on into the wee hours of the night recapping old outlaw tales with our newfound friends.

By dawn, the Tinker thieves were packing up to head on their way. I watched closely as they gathered their belongings, and I stared at the woman from the night before bathing naked in the cool water of the creek nearby. She was majestic—captivating. I tried not to let her see me, but she turned and held me with her eyes. Gliding up out of the water, she seemed to walk on the air as she made her way right for me. Out of sheer stubbornness I refused to let her see my fear. She snatched her clothes from the ground and shook them until her most-prized possession fell onto the ground in front of me.

"Go on. You keep it." Eyes wide, I smiled and picked it up. Looking up to say thanks, I realized she was already gone. I did a sweep of the area. Nowhere. Jumping up, I flipped my head down and wrapped the dark red bandanna in my hair just as I had seen her do it and ran off to find Daddy.

Daddy said that it was considered a welcoming into their tribe of bandits. I gave him a sideways turn of my head in confusion. "Daddy, I thought I was an outlaw? They are not going to take me with them, are they?"

Chuckling, he said, "Daughter, you truly are my little girl!"

Chapter 4

Daddy did not really like telling us where we were going. Not sure if it was because he did not want us to know in case we got pulled over by the laws or if he was just driving and did not have a preset destination in mind. Either way, we learned early on not to ask too many questions. I spent a lot of time looking out the windows trying to recognize landmarks or read the signs. We had already been to quite a few states in our lifetime, all along the West Coast and southern regions of the United States. So I have started to remember significant things about each one. I knew we were in California and heading north. As far as anything else, for example, where we were going to stop was not something anyone of us could have ever guessed; accurately, that is.

This time Daddy wound up in Oregon. It was a dairy farm not too far from the ocean. We pulled into the drive of a farm that smelled so bad from the manure that it made you almost sick if you did not hold your breath. As he pulled the car around the line of trailers to the right, there was a fat, old man standing there in blue jean overalls. His hair was white, and he was chewing on something that made his cheek puff out to one side like a chipmunk. He was standing next to a teenage boy with black hair and green eyes with long black eye-lashes wearing a red flannel button-up shirt. They stood watching us as we bounced the old station wagon along the graveled road. I found myself staring at the teenage boy. He was handsome, no doubt.

Daddy put the car in park alongside the pair of farmers and pushed his way out the door. I could only hear parts of what they were saying, but they were pointing around the farm and toward the trailers that we had passed on the way up the drive. I knew right away that Daddy was hustling an agreement to work for what he called "room and board." Not sure what *board* meant, but I figured out the *room* part. I recall thinking, as we made our way through the Oregon pasture-filled back roads, "God, please don't let us have to live somewhere that smells like this." Well, it did not smell like that. It was ten thousand times worse. Daddy just became the hand at a dairy farm.

We all moved into the second trailer on the right. It was not that old, but it sure looked it on the outside from all the dirt and the crappy handmade wooden steps that led to the front door. Inside everything was modern for the eighties. We had paneling on the walls, laminated tile floors in the kitchen, shag carpet for the rest of the house, and those speckled covered countertops. We had one bedroom for all the kids and one for Daddy and the Wicked Witch. There was a small, graveled parking space in front of the steps to the front door and a slightly longer graveled road that led to a wooden bunkhouse that had single-bed rooms in it, each with their own front door. Kind of like one of the old hotels Daddy had us stay in once. There was a wooden walkway that went the length of it and a huge wooden structure that looked like a barn but just covered the road the length of the bunkhouse walkway. It had extra room on the opposite side to park trucks and trailers. Down a dirt road to the left, just passed the bunkhouse, was the place Daddy said where *the magic happened.*

That night we were told to settle in and be ready early in the morning. I was always ready though. Nowadays you never knew what to expect. It kept me on my toes, and I slept so light that a cricket would make me jump up from my sleep. In the morning Daddy woke us up and explained that we could come watch what he was going to be doing all day. I eagerly put on my shoes and went to see if we had any food. I ended up being the only one of us kids that went with Daddy that day. After a few hours surrounded by cow patties and mud that smelled worse than dog crap, I got the feeling I should have stayed in bed with the rest of them.

You see, Daddy never made any permanent plans. He did not believe in the idea that he was not allowed to change his mind. So we could have packed everything and drove halfway up the West Coast just for a job he would relieve himself of in a matter of moments. I do not even know why he tried working what he called "square jobs" because he did not agree with taking orders or having any kind of routine. Damn sure, did not do a work schedule, whatever that thing was. I was tired, hungry, and had to pee, really bad, so I asked for permission to walk back to the trailer on my own. It was not an exceptionally long walk, but on the way, I came upon that young man that was standing by the owner of the dairy farm the day before. He was sitting on the porch out front of his boarding room in a rocking chair. I wondered if that was where they got that *board* part of Daddy's *room and board* from. Probably not, because why would anyone want to say the same thing twice? "Room and room?" No. I'll have to remember to ask Daddy later. His hair was slicked backward, and he had a short sleeve button-up shirt on, of which he left hanging open. He was sipping on a red-and-white Budweiser can while he smoked a cigarette he had just rolled.

As I was walking toward him, he watched me very carefully. I was not sure of his mind-set, so I just stayed on the opposite side of the bungalow and kept walking toward our place. I knew that when people drank alcohol, they made very poor decisions, but not on purpose. It was always like you were dealing with someone else. You just could not trust them. You could not know someone all of your life and know for certain that they would be that same person after drinking all day. That especially applied to people who drank beer. They will just keep drinking it like soda pop, and before they or anyone else knew it, they were drunk. Next day, they would have a really bad headache and ask questions about what happened the night before. I would listen to people explain some horrific act of atrocity to them as they tried to recall it and sat in shock as they did their damnedest to picture themselves carrying out such an event.

But sometimes, in the morning, after someone has been drinking, no one says anything about the night before because everyone involved remembers, and we are left with more of what you call "our little secrets." Those nights are hard to forget sometimes no matter how much you try. Because through it all, PTSD will always remember. It will remind me to steer clear, pay attention, and not smoke too much on the joint that they pass before bedtime. Oh, and always take note of the number of drinks someone else is having.

Today appeared to be normal enough, for the most part. As I walked by that boy, he smiled at me. His teeth were perfect, and he had a devious grin on his face. Kind of flirty. He jumped up out of his chair and jogged on over to introduce himself. Now, I am well aware of the fact that I am not his age, but that never stops them. Did not then, and never really has either. I did not talk to strangers, especially guys. But since Daddy worked there, I did not really see anything wrong with greeting him back. Besides, he was the kind of cute that made your stomach do somersaults, and I was curious on what a boy like him would have to say to someone like me.

He did not seem to be the violent type while he was intoxicated. He smiled the whole time. We talked while we walked up the drive. He asked a lot of questions and seemed extremely interested in all the answers. He giggled every time I talked. He said he loved my accent. I never really noticed I even had one.

He had taken me all the way back to our trailer so I could run in and pee; then, we were going to go back over to the barn covering that was set over the road where he parked. All he kept talking to me about was his new truck. By the way he had spoken, he had gotten a brand-new vehicle. That was not the case as I rounded the left-hand entrance. It was a beat-up old Ford pick-up truck that barely ran. The outside was painted white, but so old that it was chipping and peeling all over and had rust stains all along the bottom and the hood. I have seen worse, but he was so excited that I did not want to say much, so I just smiled.

On and on he went as he lifted the hood and proceeded to explain to me about the engine. His smile was something else. Wicked and mesmerizing. Opening the door for me on the passenger side, I climbed up into the seat. Slamming the door closed, he skipped to the driver's side and joined me in the front seat. He told me that it was okay to sit closer to him, so I slid across.

I may have been incredibly young, but I had already learned when a boy was interested in me. My body had begun reacting differently toward the opposite gender ever since the first time I was touched by one. I was only slightly uncomfortable until it turned into something that caused an indescribable feeling inside of me. I know most folks may not understand, but that is when I realized that I really did *want it* like he said. I guess that is why I never really told Daddy. Those were the kind of secrets you keep to yourself. For different reasons. The ones that would tear your family apart. Not how someone would imagine, though. If Daddy finds out, he would kill them. If Daddy kills them, he might end up in jail, but we would all have to move again. That is for sure.

When he first pressed his lips to mine, I could smell the beer before he put his tongue in my mouth. I do not exactly care for the taste either, but it did not bother me. We sat there kissing for a good while. Now, I should have paid more attention to how long we had spent talking about the truck. I am not sure how far away Daddy was when he realized it was me or precisely how long he watched that boy kiss me, but I do know that the poor kid never saw Daddy coming. He yelled for me to get out of the truck immediately, so I did my best to obey. I knew he was pissed off pretty bad, so the last thing that I was going to do was turn my back on him. I saw Daddy reach through the window of the truck and snatch that boy up by each side of his button-up shirt. Then he proceeded to jerk him straight out the window like he weighed the same as a sack of potatoes. I could tell right then this was about to be bad, really bad. The boy was cute and all but not worth dying for, so when Daddy told me, "Go home now," well, you better believe that is what I did.

The Witch did not seem like she was interested in what I was trying to explain to her, until she heard the kid screaming bloody murder. She stood up and darted for the window, grabbed a bunch of our stuff together, and told us all to load up in the backseat of the car. I saw Sissy counting our heads as we loaded up, and then she ran back in to help her. We got pretty quick at moving at the last second and we had not had time to unpack yet, so it went smoother this time. She jumped in the driver's seat, started the car, and worked our way toward Daddy.

By the time we got there, the whole board house was out on the porch watching. The old white-haired farmer was running down the road, purple-headed and winded. He probably never ran a day in his life, but that day, he was coming for Daddy like Daddy came for that boy. That was when I knew it definitely had to have been his grandson. Dropping the farm boy on the gravel, Daddy made his way to us at a hurried pace but did not do his usual Bo Duke hood slide across the front of the car, so I knew he was still really upset and, more than likely, it was at me. We made it out of there that day without the cops being involved or getting shot, which I thought was great. Though Daddy was mad about losing the new job and having to turn around and move again, he did not give me an ass-whooping that day. He just kept asking if I was okay. That was when it dawned on me. Daddy had no idea. It was all my fault. I think I will keep that one to myself as well.

Chapter 5

Oregon was a very eventful state for all of us children. I am not sure how we survived it. Sissy got bit by a black widow spider down on a pier that hung over the ocean. Now, I was not certain if those kinds of spiders were even native to the state or not, but sure enough, it was a real, live, black widow. Daddy scooped it up into an old Mason jar to show it to the doctors at the emergency room when we rushed her to the hospital. The other thing I did not like about the ocean there was that you could not swim at certain times because the tide brought little bugs with it that would burrow up under your skin and make themselves comfortable. They left little red dots on your skin and looked like chigger bites. We put fingernail polish on them to get rid of them, just like chiggers.

When Sissy got out of the hospital from the spider bite, we headed onward. Somewhere deeper into the wooded region of the state, Daddy found us a trailer park. We moved into a double-wide home right in the middle of the park. Next door lived two older women. They were identical twins, even had matching names—Isabelle and Annabelle, if I can recall accurately. Sissy took to them right away, and they seemed to do the same with her. Before long, she was out on their porch, with a plug of that chew in the foil pack that had an Indian on the front of the package in her mouth. They even taught her how to spit in the can on the steps from the swing. She was grown enough that Daddy did not seem to mind. I think he really did not care because he was not the one paying for it. I sure wish he would let me smoke a cigarette. It was getting harder and harder to go long periods of time without a butt to smoke or a cigarette I could bum or steal from somewhere else.

That and when Daddy did not work, he was always there. Maybe not right there with us, but always around somewhere. Once Daddy got a job, the Witch went and got herself one too. She just worked in the office at the trailer park, but she was not allowed to have us coming in and out all the time. She was told not to leave us unattended, though. This meant that Daddy had to pay for a sitter.

We had met some kids around the park that played with some other kids from a trailer on some land just on the other side of the park's fence. So they were literally on the backside of our trailer. Their dad had agreed to take us in for a smaller fee than the local daycare, and Daddy went to have his talk with the man.

After a few beers and a full day of bullshitting, Daddy seemed pleased enough to agree on him watching us while they worked. That guy gave me the creeps though, and I tried my best to steer clear of him, which, in turn, ended up being not that difficult after all. He let us run amuck outside all day until one of our parents showed up, called us over the fence to come home, or hollered that dinner was ready.

I liked our little system. His kids were all right to play with, and they seemed just as tough as we were. I lay in bed one night thinking of the day to come and started wondering. I know why we were tough like that, but I would sure like to know what made them hard as nails and meaner than a copperhead snake. Once I found that out, I remember thinking back to that moment in my bed and wanting to kick myself.

It was about a month into living there that it began. Now, I cannot say I did not see something coming, but I guess I had just gotten comfortable because *it* had not happened yet. Their dad drank a lot, which I always pay attention to because of previous situations where I had to deal with intoxicated people. But when you are outside playing all day, it is hard to judge how much someone inside has consumed in the last four or five hours. I did, however, notice that he had started earlier than normal. I did not know then that liquor was also being pounded like water.

Even at my age, I was well aware of the difference between liquor and beer. Though they are both alcohols, the effect they have on folks is or can be completely and mostly tragically opposite. Liquor with beer, though, and always, depending on which came first in the process, is what mattered most. I believe in the saying "Liquor before beer…never fear. Beer before liquor…never sicker." And it appeared to be accurate, so far. If they started with liquor, then they would transform into fearless monsters. If they began with beer, they would, mostly, irritate everyone, throw up a few times, and pass out at the end of the night or when the alcohol ran out. Either way, it was not anything anyone around them chose to participate in willingly. Kids, almost always, seemed to get the shorter end of that stick, literally and proverbially.

Our days of running amuck came to the end of a fairly good run that treacherous afternoon. The sun beat upon us all morning, as we ran wild in the field and climbed up and over the fences and trees on the land surrounding their trailer. By lunchtime, I was starving and, once again, had to pee really bad. Since it was normal for us to come in and out to use the bathroom, I never really questioned to ask or bring anyone else with me. All the other kids were caught up in a game of "Kill the Carrier" anyway. I remember opening the door with caution because I was nervous. The trailer had rays of light that shown through the blinds into the unlit living area like fairy dust carrying tiny little Sprites into the hidden secrets beyond. It was creepy but almost magical at the same time. I slipped quickly down the hall, feeling my way along the wall as I guided myself toward the bathroom. Normally, when it is dark inside, after someone has been drinking, it means that they have finally done us all a favor and passed out cold. I crept into the tiny boxlike room and did my business expeditiously.

I had not found the value of being alone in the dark with myself or anyone else, for that matter, at this particular time in my life. I knew that bad things happened, but most of all, they tended to happen in the dark. Well, to me, they did. That is when the darkness in people shows itself the most. I believe it calls to us, the darkness. It whispers its promises of grandeur, fame, fortune, adventure, fantasy, and satisfaction. It entices the heart's lust for the flesh of this world. It beckons to the beast within us. It sniffs at the air for the aroma of another demon's spirit. I understood it; I was just not used to it yet. I say, *yet* because I could definitely feel the evil arising in me. And if I could feel it in me, I knew that other people who had already chose to take hold of it had no problems unleashing it in them. Walking out into the hall, I felt the sting, sharp and cold, like the metal itself. Repeatedly. I did my best to block every one of the blows from his hand, but he got me every time with that coat hanger. A coat hanger does not sound like much, but it is small and thin. It will whip you like a switch, and it hurts bad enough to leave a memory—one that will remind you to dodge it the next time.

Backing up, as I dipped and ducked as quickly as I could, abruptly ended when I fell backward onto the couch at the end of the living room. I had run out of space and was now trapped. I felt the heat from the tears pouring out of my eyes and cried out for him to stop. When he heard me, he shook his head like he was not aware that someone else was in the room and looked at me in confusion. Then he caught himself and snapped for me to *remain on the couch* without another word out of me. You better believe that he was granted his demands.

Sissy came looking for me, toward the end of the day, when we were called home. I did not have it in me to explain what had happened, so I just said that he told me that I was to remain on the couch. She just looked at me strange and grabbed my hand to lead me out. Doing my best, I held in the pain from the hanger welts and made my way back to our trailer without another word. Their dad was nowhere to be seen.

The following day, our routine was a whole new ballgame. Every one of the kids in my family was told to line up on the couch. Their oldest son was in charge of the fly swatter, leather strap, and coat hanger. They had now become the rod of truth, and he the unlawful enforcer. What had we done? The thought left when I saw their dad crack open another beer. It was not us. I knew that.

It was the taste of blood that that man got from the day before when he realized that there were no repercussions this morning.

I should have said something, but I did not want Daddy to lose another job or us to move again, and all because of me.

Why did it always have to happen to me? A kid can only take on so much damn blame a beating can give before there has to be some kind of break. Unfortunately, for me, I feel the break will come long before the actual reprieve. Sure enough, I was right. The day came when Daddy was let out of work early for personal reasons, or should I say, he *quit*. There is something Daddy never got, and that was *fired* or *laid off*. Mainly because he always "beat them to the punch," as he liked to say. I am no expert, but I think, he would just get sick and tired of having no fun. I know I would. That particular afternoon, though, I believe Daddy was right on time with this whole *quitting* business. He squeezed through the crack in the fence and wandered up on the porch looking for us. He had said *it was not normal* for us to be inside instead of out in the yard raising hell. When he crept onto the steps, he could see us all lined along the couch at the back end of the trailer. He pointed his finger at Sissy and motioned for her to "Come here." When Sissy hesitated and looked back to the chair in the middle of the room that held the overweight, intoxicated, abusive babysitter, Daddy pushed the door smooth in, only he used his foot and maybe a little bit of force as well.

The guy was so drunk, he did not even budge or drop the leather strap he had clenched between his fists. The sound startled the rest of us quite a bit, though, and we knew it was coming. I guessed by the look in Daddy's eyes when Sissy would not move.

Daddy took a look around, then gave Sissy instructions to evacuate all the children, even the other ones. Of course, we jumped on the opportunity to finally be released from the grasps of the dirty, sweat-ridden couch that had held us captive for the last three weeks straight.

I was praying Daddy did not go back to jail, but I was kind of hoping for a little more physical retribution. Like I have stated before, Daddy was a very calculated individual, who thought everything out prior to, not because he was worried about consequences but because he wanted to figure out how he would benefit most from each circumstance—normally! On the other hand, when it came to a justifiable reason to hurt someone legally and get away with it, he knew it was always going to be behind us kids. So when he did not perform as I had no doubt, whatsoever, he would; it took me by surprise. Daddy had another card up his sleeve for this occasion. Another trick, so to speak. We had never been in this exact situation prior to now, so we could not possibly know what he was up to.

Daddy may have destroyed that guy's trailer something good, but afterward, he just walked out and let the grease ball make it! I could not believe my eyes and ears. Or even that I was not dreaming this whole thing up. Once we all were home, Daddy demanded to hear all our sides of the story. Sissy told hers. I watched Bubba and Hellion explain their version, and I recited mine. It all began with me. I knew that. I did not want him to, but it was useless trying to lie about it because I knew it would eventually come to light.

The very next day, Daddy had us sit down so that he could go over the events that had transpired since we had been sleeping. Apparently, it is against the law to abuse children, but you can, technically, sue them for monetary value if it is in an environment that is considered a *business*. This type of business being related to the childcare industry. Babysitting is considered independent contracting or self-employment in this circumstance. Daddy had done some research and filed a petition in civil court as well and made a phoned-in police report and filed a protective order, considering the man lived in such close range of our residence.

Sissy had been nominated to testify by Daddy because he felt she was old enough to articulate the details better. The more details, trauma, dramatics, or shall I say, "fake tears," the more financial payout will be rewarded to the petitioner. I had no idea what any of that shit meant, except this: I did not have to go in front of all those people in the court room and describe or, shall I say, "relive" all that horrific crap that I had done me damnedest to forget to begin with.

The day they went to court, they loaded into the car and drove away. I remember the look on her face. She seemed like she wanted to ralph violently but was so afraid to open her mouth that she had been quiet all morning long. Sissy was not the kind to show fear, so it shocked me until I heard Daddy say what he had said to her as they backed out the drive. I kept thinking that I should run after the car and beg him to take me instead, that I could do a better job explaining everything, but I knew it would not have changed his mind or made a bit of difference in his eyes. He had made his choice. They had spent hours practicing with the lawyer, and Daddy was confident in her abilities. What he failed to realize, though, is the minute he threatened her with his "You better not fuck this up for me!" he had already screwed himself.

Later took longer than ever to arrive. I sat waiting; it seemed like days but was only barely over an hour. I walked around the trailer park looking for something to get into or keep me occupied until they returned. Nothing I did could keep the scene in my head from playing over and over again. I was worried about Sissy. It was not needless worrying, either, because I knew what I was seeing was not just a guess.

I was what Daddy called *gifted*. I had something people call a third eye or visions. I also heard and felt things that other people could not. I am in tune with a world that most do not even know exists. I describe these facts as *pictures of knowledge* or the *voice in my ear*. The other world is a spiritual realm of some sort. The holy dead and the shadows of demons in between. When I get these pictures, the way I did this day, I could not deny or change what was about to take place. I only have the ability to prepare for the aftermath.

When the time I had been counting down to arrived, I could feel them coming from up the road. What I felt was the heat from Sissy's insides—her hurt and anger. She was not sorry she made Daddy lose that settlement. Her hate radiated into me like fire. Daddy had no idea that she had done it on purpose. He assumed that she just choked up in front of all those people in the courtroom.

As they pulled into the driveway, she remained quiet and kept her head down like she was in fear of him. It worked. Daddy dragged her by her hair kicking and screaming into the trailer, and as he passed me, he mumbled, "I should've taken you." I remained silent and stayed on the steps as I tried my best not to imagine the torture that she had willingly put herself through just to get back at Daddy.

The only thing that reassured me that everything was going to be okay was the smile on her face as she winked at me when he was hauling her inside like a rag doll. I thought to myself about all the times I had wanted to do the same and just did not have the nerve. I loved Daddy, but if there was anything he taught us, it was "Sometimes, people did not deserve to get what they wanted" and "Others needed to remember that every dog has its day." Though you would never believe it by the nightmare of sounds coming from our house that night, but Sissy had won.

Chapter 6

After the judgment of that lawsuit went against Daddy and the whole neighborhood caught wind of it, we were on the road. This time Daddy foresaw a need to change vehicles. I remember how excited he was because it was an old blue pickup truck with a camper on the bed of it. When I say camper, I am saying a home on top of a truck that was not, originally, on the truck. It was like an RV, but the live-in part could not be accessed from the cab, and it could be removed from the bed if need be. There was a door on the back that lined up with the tailgate. Now, no one was allowed to ride in the back while the truck was moving, but we we're not all going to fit in the front seat of the pickup now, were we?

Daddy sure did come up with all kinds of new ideas for where and how to live while we were "traveling," so to speak. I think it was more like "running," but I would sure as hell would *never* say that shit out loud. Not because I was afraid Daddy would be upset because he was embarrassed. I knew that he was proud to be a fugitive, but I would get my ass whooped if someone overheard and tried to turn him in to the law.

Daddy had a special phrase we were to shout out loud if we saw a cop. It was "Uh-oh, spaghetti o's." We were told never to use it unless we were 100 percent certain that it was some sort of law enforcement officer. There was only one of us that ever used it in another situation, and I am grateful to be alive to tell anyone about it.

You see, we had stopped at a rest stop for the night once, when it was winter. It had gotten so cold that we were all wrapped up warm and snuggling in pile of blankets in the back of the ole Oldsmobile. It was a tank of a car, big solid steel body with the white roof and heavy, metal doors. Back then, doors like that broke anything that was accidentally slammed in one, hood included.

I had to use the bathroom, and if you know anything about me by now, you know this is where the trouble begins. Hell, one would assume that by now I would have a healthy fear of peeing, but even after years of traumatic stories that all start with "I had to pee really bad and..." I am absolutely free from any bathroom-related issues, except the shower.

I was attempting to climb out of the back passenger door while still wrapped in as many covers as possible, a smaller blanket snug around my waist. Sliding out of the door, Sissy reached up and slammed it quickly behind me, as to not lose any of the heat we had worked so hard to build up. All the windows were fogged up pretty hard, and they had been jamming to "Shout at the Devil" on the eight-track player Daddy had installed earlier that weekend so not one person could hear or see my screams once Sissy locked that door in place. Funny thing is, I was caught in a manner that I could not just turn and beat my fists on the window, or I would have. No, my left butt cheek was squashed tighter than a jelly jar in between the car and the back door. In the midst of all my pain and panic, the only thing that I could come up with was to scream "Uh-oh, spaghetti o's" at the top of my lungs. It was great that I did because Daddy heard that instantly.

As he did a sweep of the rest stop, I saw him realize that there was not any cop about to roll up on him, unsuspectingly. It was just one of his kids needing an ass-whooping for fibbing or making him panic. He looked around the car to see who it was, as he adjusted the volume dial on the radio. Counting heads, he did a retake. "Where's Daughter?" I heard him shouting. I just kept hollering that phrase as loud as I could, but the cold, winter wind seemed to steal the sound right out of my mouth.

I kept wondering how not one single person even thought to come help that was watching the scene in the parking lot from the comfort and warmth of their own vehicles. Who does that?

I recall Sissy finally looking up to see me at the window glaring through the fog-filled glass and only opening the door and jerking me in because she wanted to stay warm. I was leaking a few tears still, and my bottom lip was trembling against my will. Bubba asked if I was all right, right about the time Daddy yanked me up out the same door that Sissy had just jerked me through. Does anyone in my family know how to communicate in any way other than physically? I wonder. As Daddy snatched me in the air and proceeded to thoroughly enlighten me on how we *do not* say that unless we are serious, he pulled the backside of my pants down around my knees. Then he just dropped me right there on the concrete next to the car. He got really quiet, then instructed me to roll back over on my stomach so he could get a better view of the mark that heavy metal made after it had pinned my cheek for a good three to five minutes.

My butt suffered serious damage from that horrible episode. Bad enough to deter a beating from Daddy and bad enough to leave a permanent reminder. It was on the top, left cheek and kind of looked like a birthmark with three freckles.

At thirty-three years of age, I counted thirty-three freckles in total. I guess that was the "one to grow on" deal with the birthday spankings that people never forget. I was not sure if I was right, but I do know that the scar got me out of the horror Daddy was planning on sharing with me. It makes me smile because if you think about it, I still got my butt handed to me in one way, shape, or form, I reckon.

Chapter 7

On our way across the states, we made a few essential stops to some familiar faces, friends, and relatives. Well, back then, we were always told that everyone was a relative of some sort, mostly aunts and uncles. Mainly because all outlaws are related. I think it was also due to the fact that there were so many to keep up with that it was easier for us kids to remember. All girls were aunts, and all men were uncles. In case we had to identify them in public, it looks less suspicious, especially if we were out in large numbers. It'd just be a "family reunion."

I once asked Daddy what jail was like, and that was the way he described it. It did not make sense until later when I was first arrested and earned my own badge of honor, those stripes an outlaw either fears or wears with pride. The fear only comes from understanding now the laws know who they really are, and the pride is knowing not only do the laws know, but so do the outlaws. With open arms, we welcome you into the family. Henceforth, Daddy's idea of it. That and a true outlaw will probably know at least a handful of brothers and sisters at any given facility they frequent. So getting arrested was just a free escort to our "family reunion." It was like a "welcome-home" vacation package paid for by no other than the laws themselves. Is that not irony at its finest?

If you look back on your life to the way you were raised, the values that you were taught, and the moral fiber by which you hold the standards of the world around you to today, you might see how our universes were extremely different than each other's. I am not sure Daddy even raised us like this to be better people in his world or if he just taught us the stuff that would benefit him in the long run.

But I looked upon my life, and this is what I noticed. I was groomed, shaped, and transformed intentionally, regardless of why, to be able to handle the most God-awful trauma one human can manage in ten lifetimes. Despite the disaster of circumstances that I have endured, I have gotten over it all, still with the ability to accept any and all situations and move forward without looking back. Now, I am not saying that I do not seek revenge or that I just allow people to be any kind of way without doing my best to enlighten their reality with a healthy dose of my very extensive imagination. What I am saying is I can handle anything and anyone, at any time, in any manner, that best benefits, suits, or behooves me or anyone else, that I may love or respect. Whether it has any negative impact does not matter at this point. On the larger scheme of things, if it helps me in any way, it is most definitely going to be a positive for those that are in my life on a permanent level.

The world has been changing, though, ever so slightly since I was a kid. It reminds me of the thorny thicket. You see, it used to be like this: close to God, family, and friends. Always included good wholesome values such as honor, loyalty, respect, self-discipline, integrity, and so forth. People spent time with one another, had manners, were taught etiquette, went to church, learned about God, and went out of their way to help each other for no reason and without repayment or expectations. Somewhere along the way, someone opened a door by accepting one evil thing to be okay.

Like someone decided that they were going to cuss, and afterward, they did it again and again, until it was all right with them, and then the people around them accepted it too. But cussing was not enough because now everyone did it, so it was "normal". Then someone else started smoking cigarettes, and they introduced it into the world the exact same way. And this went on and on and on until the world and everyone in it had eventually become okay with all of the things designed to destroy it. The world had basically accepted the poison as food, and their children were so immune to it that they never noticed that what they were consuming was rotten. I came from a generation which was not completely desensitized, but my siblings and I were forced to eat the poison, even though we knew it was bad. What choice did we have? It was all we had to eat! Outlaw for breakfast, outlaw for lunch, and outlaw for supper to finish us up.

We were not the first to be contaminated by the flesh and sin of others' ideas of revolution, and we, damn sure, would not be the last. You can see the sin in all the lives around you every day now. It is common, the average, normal. Dare one, even, guess if one is a Christian? (Without fear of persecution oneself.) Though the point remains. We will all be outlaws bleeding the stench of rot and death before the God of us all comes to reign hell's fury upon us.

Chapter 8

You would think that a family who lived in a car would have no earthly business owning any kind of pet or animal. Though we did have a rat, which Daddy decided to name Charlie, living in our trunk and eating holes in our clothes and food. That is not the particular one I speak of when I say that Daddy did not necessarily share the same concept of pet ownership.

I recall the day we acquired King. He was a Timber Wolfe puppy that had wandered out of the hills and into an apartment complex. Daddy had stopped to score going through the north country, somewhere outside Washington state to the east. Everyone was hanging out and bullshitting. Every so often, there would be some kind of yelp, and then you would hear this jiggling of the door. It almost sounded as if a kid or lady was being hurt. Now I know you are probably thinking that after hearing a noise like that, someone should have gone outside and checked on their well-being the first time. But if you all have warrants or aliases, you just leave it to good Samaritans. Trust me, there is always a hero in the bunch. Then there was actually a knock on the door and one of the brothers announced themselves, so somebody took it upon themselves to open it and let them inside. As he entered, walking in behind him was what appeared to be a puppy at first glance or to a kid my age anyway. Daddy jumped up out of his seat and scooped up the whelp. He peaked his head out, shook his head, turned back, and reported, "Nothing, not a single soul or bitch anywhere." So he closed and locked the door.

These apartments were kind of out by themselves, but not so far out that a Grey Wolfe pup would be able to wander from its mom without it noticing before it had run too far off. How exactly King had arrived that day remains a mystery, but Daddy needed no reason. King was his, and that was that! That animal was of value in more ways than one to him, and I could feel his excitement from across the living room.

The guy that had come in was the guy that everyone had been waiting for, so after Daddy had his chance to speak with him in the back room, we got to leave. He was still clutching the damn thing as we got back to the car and all the way back to the motel where the Witch and the rest of the kids were checking out. Do not get me wrong; puppies and stuff were cool and all, but I was not exactly sure how it was all going to end up working out. It did not seem like anyone else had the same thought as I did, not even in the back of their minds.

I guess you get so tired of not being able to enjoy the kid stuff that a chance at having a puppy is like winning the lottery or waking up in the same place every morning. Daddy had already named him, so there were no chances of us fighting over a name or ending up with some stupid kid name like "Happy" or "Jake." It was a name of position in our clan, and I knew it. Daddy said he was now part of the family. It was obvious, he was going to be the priority from now on—food, attention, responsibility. No one else seemed to notice. How were they so blind? He was Daddy's dog, and it said it all in his name. I was only Daughter, but he was King… Outlaw.

Daddy spent more time than imaginable with that damn thing. Though I will give King credit. He was smart. He was as big as a small horse once he became full-grown. I know because Daddy had taught him to let us ride on his back. His size and thick coat also served us kids as a blanket in the cold. He would climb to the top bunk over the cab that held our bed and sleep across every one of us to keep us warm. He and the Chow we acquired along the way named Rambo. That was until we had to leave them somewhere in New Mexico along our endless journey, right along with our damn camper.

Chapter 9

Flea markets were a really huge ordeal when we were growing up. It gave Daddy a way to boost all kinds of necessities or knick-knacks that we would need for one reason or another. Either on an upcoming job, to scope out the next, or all sorts of survival items. This was also the opportunity he took to make us see how much he cared. He would surprise us and pull out a wad of cash. He would hand each one of us a bill or two, normally a five or ten. Back in those days, the value of a dollar seemed like it held more clout.

Every single thing I have ever gained in my life was always earned in some way, shape, or form. Be it by blood, sweat, tears, or one of Daddy's good old-fashioned chess games, we were just pawns. Daddy's idea of flea market shopping with us kids had mainly one or more of three intentions, or shall we say, goals: panhandling, distraction, or it babysat us for him while he went and found some drugs or "shit to get into." We were trained by a professional, though, so it was no big feat for any of us. I am not sure about Sissy or the boys, but for me, it was a vacation from the customary jobs he had us doing. The others felt more like slave labor and seemed as if they violated some kind of child labor laws. I am not quite sure those really existed to anyone in the world I grew up in, though.

This particular flea market was where I found out who Janis Joplin was or, at least, what her music sounded like. I was dragging along through the tented tables of curious delight when I backed into a hippie with headphones on and jacked into an eight-track player. The woman next to him was standing there doing the same

thing, except she was grooving to the beat of whatever melody was chiming through the oversized earmuffs attached to her head. They both resembled alien life-forms I had seen in a movie once or twice, glowing in all their technological glory.

I found myself wandering over the array of vinyl and eight-tracks, one after another, from Pink Floyd to Jimmy Hendrix. Then there she sat, sprawled behind the handlebars of a motorcycle. I read the cover: *Janis Joplin Greatest Hits*. I cannot help myself. I pulled it from the place in the rack and walked over to where the hippie had laid the earphones. I had extensive knowledge on eight-track players because of Daddy's. He would make us DJ while he drove the car if the Witch was not riding next to him. I removed the tape that was in the deck from the last session and slipped in the tape from the rack. I slid on the headphones and readjusted them to fit my head as best they could for a kid my age. When I hit the play button and the music blared loudly into my ears, I was in a trance, losing myself into the sensation of sound pouring into my soul. And there went the chorus: "Take it, take another little piece of my heart now, baby." I took out the tape from the unit and walked over to the lady to purchase it. She went on to say that she was sold out of the eight-track tapes but had a different type of tape she could sell me for just five dollars. It was called a cassette tape. She asked if I knew which type of deck was in my parents' vehicle. I looked at her, kind of offensively, and directed my eyes toward my hand holding the eight-track. She smiled and handed me the cassette, snatched the eight-track, and took my five off of the table. Then she sent me on my way because I was keeping her from the line of customers behind me. I turned to see two adults standing together.

As she shooed me on my way, I started to get upset. I knew that cassette was not going to fit. I went to interrupt her current sell and got shut down. I thought to myself, *This bitch! She does not want to listen to me, then she can listen to Daddy*. If there was one thing that I loved about Daddy's temper, it was when it was directed at someone else, and more specifically, someone that tried to bulldoze or strong arm me or my brothers or sister.

I spent a good hour searching that damn flea market for Daddy. Ironically, by the time I found him, he was standing at the same table speaking with that wench that tried to hustle me. My entire face lit up when I noticed the cassette player in his hand. I knew right away that it was the same one that I needed to run the tape I was holding. She saw me coming and made the worst damn assumption she could have made. As I pushed my way through the crowd, she began saying some crazy stuff about "wild-ass kids with parents that don't keep them on a damn leash" and pointed right in my direction. Ha, stupid lady! Daddy turned just in time for me to reach up for his hand. After that, well, I really did not have to say anything. Her big mouth did it all before I got there.

Once it dawned on her that he was that parent with "the wild-ass kid," it was way too late to stop the situation unfolding before her. You see, Daddy had caught on before he even turned to look. I imagine from previous events featuring "wild-ass kids" always meaning his. Either that or he had seen his air and opportunity and seized it. No matter why, he now had a reason to shove that cassette deck in the back of his pants and proceed to act a fool behind his darling little girl, who was just swindled by the treacherous flea-market-vendor lady.

The rack, where I had found Janis in all her mysterious wonder, was the first to go. Then the table directly in front of that wretched woman. I found my chance to do my part when Daddy showed his back to me. Snatching a folded bag from the concrete, I pulled the car audio device from his jeans and dropped it into the sack. I began to dip in and around the onlookers until I reached a clearing in the back of the crowd. I made my way through the parking lot and found the Witch sitting on the hood puffing a joint and blowing the smoke in Baby Girl's face as she rocked her to sleep. She noticed me hauling ass through the lot and motioned for me to just put whatever I had stolen in the truck. I watched her scan the area. Bubba, Hellion, and Sissy were heading right for us with hands full as well.

It was not until she caught a glimpse of Daddy at top speed that she got off her ass and grabbed her belongings off the hood. By the time he made it to the middle of the parking lot, she had already pulled the truck up alongside him, and he jumped inside. The rest of us were peeking through the blinds of the camper on the back.

I will give the Witch this much; she was down for Daddy like eighteen flats on a big rig. Looking down at the scars on my arms from the last cigarette burns, I thought about how other kids' moms were. I wondered if they were all only good to the dads and bad to the kids. Hell, our real mama left us standing in the lobby of an office holding a note for Daddy as we waited for him to get off work that day. It was just me, Bubba, and Sissy back then, though.

When I got older, I would see the news and read the paper to see that day's horrific, child tragedies. Then I would think to myself about how grateful I was that it was not any worse. Though, I would tell my stories growing up and could see the look on the other kids' faces. They thought I was a *liar*. No one really believes that the kind of life we spoke of exists outside of the movies or news, and I never believed that it had any negative effect on me.

As I grew through each phase of life, that past trauma would yield a whole new set of barriers. Some of them impacting my life so intensely that I could find no way out or no solution. Some so subtle that I never knew that they were issues until their devastation had laid complete claim on my future and left me in utter ruins.

Chapter 10

I really liked the camper Daddy had gotten. There were all kinds of perks to having it, instead of a regular vehicle, like a car or truck. It was always cramped in any of them no matter what size they were because we had a large family, extra people, animals, and all of our belongings that traveled with us everywhere we went. Normally, if we gained any kind of extra anything, we would have to get rid of something to make room for whatever *it* may be. The only thing that we could say for certain was that nobody was going to be replaced, which was part of the family, dogs and other animals always included. Unless they happen to die, of course. Then that was the way of things, enough said. Other than that, we knew that none of the adult's stuff was going first, which only left us kids to have to decide what we wanted more than everything else. That part really sucked. It happened frequently too. So it sucked all the time. You do not really get used to something like that as a child. It just trains you for adulthood. Though, with the camper, it did not really have to happen very often. Score one for the gypsy mobile home.

The other thing about the camper that made it so great, not just for the kids but for adults too, was the fact that you did not have to stop if you had to use the bathroom. Daddy did not like stopping very much when he had somewhere to be or when we were running from the laws. In a car, you can go number one, pee in a cup or bottle, and throw it out the window. Easy enough, I suppose. Now, we just open the back door on the camper and toss it out, but the other traffic does not see you doing your business through the windows. I know you are thinking I was going to say we had a bathroom inside it. Well, we did, but Daddy had not gotten around to fixing it, so we were not allowed to use the toilet. Only have privacy. Score two for the privacy portal.

Thing I always had an issue with was going number two. You cannot do that in a cup, and if you could, I would not have. But you do not throw stuff like that out the window. It is difficult as it is tossing a cup of urine. Usually, it gets on the vehicle somehow. I could not fathom the other stuff doing that or hitting another car. Ew. Daddy would be pissed if that happened.

You see, I had to go to the bathroom really bad this one time. I know, big shock. Daddy was "putting space" between us and his last city job. I had been made to use the restroom prior to it all. Though I did use it, it just was not that way. When I saw Daddy running back to the car from the liquor store, he had just held up at gun point, it got my adrenaline pumping. My heart was racing, and I felt myself begin to tremble a little. It is never good for me when that happened because it normally stimulated everything else in me, and as always, it did this time. I should have just waited to sit up until Daddy had driven off, but I could feel his stomach tied in knots and hear his heart pounding the moment he opened the front door of the store. I was concerned because normally he was not so wound up, and I wanted to see if everything was all right. Of course, it was the same as every other time, but me lifting my head to watch it got me just as wired.

Naturally, I tried to hold it until I thought we were far enough away. When I finally said something, Daddy went on to explain that I would need to hold it just a little longer. Well, that was fine and all, but I had not told him that I had already been doing that. I have always been one of those kinds of folks that does not need to spend a whole bunch of time doing my business, so when it was time to go, it was time to go. Seeing as how it was winter and all, during this specific occasion, it made the situation that much worse because we were all cuddled up under the blankets. I was not going to make it much longer, but I was too scared to tell him. I realized there was no time left, so I began to cry. Now, outlaws do not cry, I know, or at least that was what Daddy always said. But I am telling you now, they do. I have seen them. As I leaned forward to ask once more, the words had barely came out my mouth right as he backhanded the right side of my face. Then, the other end of me decided to let loose and ruin the rest of the night.

Since I had no desire to ever speak again and what was done was done, I saw no sense in announcing the tragedy to Daddy. The rest of the kids knew exactly what had taken place because they were all in the same backseat and under the same smelly covers. Not one of them said a single word. We all sat there in silence waiting for Daddy to figure it out. Of course, they all scooted farther away, but I could not blame them. I would have done the same. We were all hoping that he would get to where we were going before he realized what I had done to his backseat and our blankets. I know Sissy was demising a plan to cover my ass already. I could see it on her face. It was not until about fifteen minutes later that Daddy decided to say something about an exit ahead for us to stop so we could use the facilities. They all must have been pretty distracted up front not to even notice what had gone wrong just inches away and trapped inside the same vehicle.

When Daddy did pull off the highway, he rolled the window down just enough to toss his cigarette butt out and shut it back. I reckon that is about the moment it went terribly bad for me. By the look on his face when he turned to me, he had become the Boogeyman again. Screeching into the gas station, he pulled up between the pump closest to the store where they let people use the water when their radiators overheated. As the car rolled to a stop, every kid had already tucked and rolled out of the car so fast that I did not have time to save myself.

Jumping out the driver's side, he whipped around the back and grabbed a hold of my wrist in one hand and the blankets in the other. He tossed them onto the ground and threw me on top. Though, not to prevent me from getting hurt intentionally, it just worked out like that. I appreciated the little things life offered. I could see the anger inside his eyes, but his rage was like a heatwave rushing through the air around him and gunning straight for me. I did not mean to do what I had done. I had no choice, but he was not going to see it like that.

He never said a word. Instead, he stomped over to the hose rolled in a pile next to the ice machine, turned the spigot, and walked toward me with evil grueling through his smile. Holy shit, that water was freezing, and the pressure from the handle was so high that it hurt when it hit my skin. It was stinging me so bad; I began to cry again. Then, in front of God and everyone, he yanked all my clothes off and hosed me down from head to toe until I was red from the sting of the water and purple from the cold.

Afterward, he left me to stand by the gas pump naked while the Witch found some clothes and he sprayed out the backseat, which left us kids with no option for warmth. Wet seat, wet blankets, and no replacements. The Witch went along with Daddy's sinister mood and handed me a pair of shorts to wear and a tee shirt so thin you could see right through it. No panties. It would not have been too odd without them. Except I was hoping I would get a pair just to warm me up a little more. I felt bad for my brothers and Sissy, who suffered with me, not a word of complaint out of any of them, even Hellion who loved to get shit started behind me. I did good to muzzle the sound of my cries but could not keep the tears from running. With the camper on the truck, though, and Daddy's makeshift bucket toilet, I would not have to ever relive that moment again. Score three for the rolling restroom.

Sissy had other events that caused her problems. She was older, so she was always the one in charge. Seems great to everyone until you are always the one in that position. That usually meant that she had to watch Baby Girl since she let us watch ourselves. Watching Baby Girl was also something that she had to do in the backseat if the Witch was driving. She hated her in the car seat upfront. She said it was *against the law*. I do not know when that ever mattered, but I think it was just an excuse to not have to pay her any mind.

One night, when we had the ole Oldsmobile still, Daddy had gotten a room for us but made her take all of us girls with her to run an errand, which meant I got to ride up front and Sissy had to sit in the back again with Baby Girl. After the run she made, we were still a good way from getting back and Sissy had finally gotten her to sleep. We had the radio up, and the Witch agreed that Sissy could sit up next to me in the middle. Getting into the front seat from the back never required us to stop the car normally, so without hesitation, Sissy began to climb over the seat that separated us. As she did, she grabbed onto the Witch's shoulder. She pushed Sissy off like some part of the ceiling had fallen onto her. It threw Sissy off balance, so she tried to regain it by wrapping her hand around the top part of the steering wheel. She caught herself, then pulled the rest of her body into the seat. The Witch had been drinking, and her reaction time was not so on time. The force that Sissy used was enough to pull the car all the way to the right. There was not another car in the lane next to us, so I am not exactly sure why she had jerked the wheel so hard in the other direction, but that sure was her excuse for crashing the car into the ditch when the tow truck guy let her call Daddy from the CB radio. The dispatch made the call but let her talk. She was short and talked in code. She said all she needed was the money to pay the driver when we got there.

Daddy was freaking pissed to the point of purple. At first, he was mad at the Witch, but she quickly adverted the blame to Sissy. I could hear them argue out front of the hotel door as we all sat on the beds waiting for the outcome. When he came through the door once more, we already knew that his sights would be on Sissy. She was trying to explain her side, but he never took our word over hers. I think it was easier for him to take it out on us, and you could tell he did not like to fight with her. It was how it always went.

Daddy had shaken Sissy so hard she ran into the bathroom to throw up, but when he heard her puking, he ran over and slammed the bathroom door shut. I did not understand why her making gagging sounds would bother him; it never has before.

That was until I saw him lock it from the outside. *Oh god*, I thought. *Who would place a lock on the outside?* As I heard her first plea and jiggle of the handle, I caught it out of the corner of my eye. The light switch. It was on the outside of the bathroom, mounted on the wall by the sink. My heart sank. He knew what he was doing. Once Daddy had flipped that switch to the off position, there was no way to save her. Hell, we were all afraid of the dark, but Sissy had something happen before I could remember that made it worse for her. The screams bellowed out of the cracks in the door like sheer horror had begun on the opposite side, like something was hurting her.

Daddy let it go on like that for the whole hour. We could not do anything but listen to her fear leaving her in pure panic. I think she clawed the back of the door so hard that she broke all of what nails she had off in it. Her fingers were literally bleeding, and she was limping, I am sure, from kicking it with the same leg over and over. Her hair was crazy and sticking up in every direction like it would if you would have stuck a key in the light socket. Though, mine never did that when I put a key in one.

She was still crying, but not out loud. And she was let to eat some pizza before she came to lie in bed with me. Every moment since she had stepped out of the darkness, I could feel the darkness rising inside of her. She was not the same. You could not tell, but I could feel it from the change in her soul. The color around her had gone and now loomed a shadow of hate. I sure bet Sissy was glad you cannot reach the steering wheel from the backseat since there is no backseat in the camper. Score four for the kid cab in the back.

And almost always, the Witch and Daddy stayed up in the front. Score five for our little home, all alone.

Chapter 11

Earth and rock crunched beneath my feet. No matter how loud the sounds of my steps or the echo of my stride rings in my ears, I continued to push forward. Row after row of tall grass rose up around me like an endless sea with no hint of direction. If I remained crouching, then maybe, just maybe, they will not be able to find me. I stopped to listen, waiting to hear any sign of the impeding pursuit. There was nothing. My breath, the only indicator of life within miles. Staying put where I was seemed like a really good idea. My heart was thumping loudly inside of my chest, and my breathing was extremely labored.

Given the chance to think finally, my mind raced. *Who are these people? What do they want? I am only a little girl. Maybe they came for me because I am an outlaw. Daddy said the day would come that every outlaw would have to run. Run? Why?* I thought. *Are they going to hunt us? Am I being hunted now? Have they taken the rest and I'm the only one left? What have they done with my family?* I want to scream, to cry out for Daddy. He would know what to do, but I know he is not going to answer…because he is not here.

A crunch of steps sounded out in the stillness of the night air, heavy and closing in on me and quickly. Breaking into a full-on run, I stammered before I gained my balance. Every inch of my body was aching. My blood was pulsing and pumping so loud that it was pushing out all of the sound around me. The grass was almost tall enough to hide me if I stand straight up, and at that point, I was not worried if they can see me. I just knew that I had to put some space between me and them. Daddy said, "If you can run, do it, and whatever you do, don't stop running. Hiding only gives them a chance to trap, surround, or find you. They will search everywhere until they find the place you hid, and they *will* find you." So I just went. Ahead I could make out a forest. It was dark enough outside that I felt sure enough that I can lose them in there. The blades whipped my face, and the dew from the damp of the darkness clang to my skin and the sweat trickling down my brow was stinging my eyes as I made for the trees. Everything was blurry, and I felt a dizzy sensation creeping and realized I was not breathing right. In through my nose, one and two. Out through my mouth, one and two. Just like Daddy said. Creating a cadence in my head, I found the safety of the forest growing closer. Whoever was at my back was hot on my heels. I looked over my shoulder and saw their hand grasping for me and threw my body into a baseball slide for home plate only to turn and gaze into the shadow of the figure before me.

The dawn was approaching and casting a dim glow of hope only to be shattered by the Shadow Man. His presence was overwhelming, and I slid right to his feet. My stomach dropped. My heart leaped into my throat. I panicked. There was nowhere to run. I flipped over onto my belly, grasping the earth with my hands to pull myself into another direction. I dug my feet into the ground, then I felt him. His hand was tight around my ankle.

"No!" I cried out. Tears were welling hard from the pit of my gut. This is not happening. Jerking and twisting, I attempted to free myself. He began to drag me by the ankle into the depths of the forest. Clawing and scratching into the dirt for something of significance, I found nothing. I was trapped. They got me.

"Daddy! Daddy! Help me, Daddy! Please, help! Daddy!"

I yanked myself up and opened my eyes. The relief I felt from the scene around me poured into me causing me to breakdown into a full-on sob. I never thought I would be relieved to hear the Witch's voice. She was reminding Hellion to shake out his clothes and check his shoes for scorpions. Then she turned to me and said, "Another one of them night terrors, Daughter?" I could do nothing but nod my head and wipe the snot from my nose with the sleeve of my shirt.

Daddy ran back into town, so I cannot climb up on him and find any consolation. I took a few minutes to gather my bearings and get out of my sleeping bag. Shaking out my clothes and shoes, I dressed and headed for the comfort of the mountain stream near camp.

Climbing upon a boulder hanging on the edge of the water, I sat and just listened—listened to water, the birds, the leaves, the sounds of life, and everything around me. It calmed me down. But I could still see him behind my eyes. It was not the first time he has been in my dreams. He was there. Always somewhere. I am not scared of much, but just his presence takes the breath right out of me and has even paralyzed my entire body. On occasion, I have pulled him right out of the nightmare with me. That was how I knew he belonged to the other dimension—the one I can see and most others cannot. Why was he haunting me like this? Tormenting me. His spirit was strong and nothing but evil. He was coming for my soul; I could feel him whispering to me, calling for it.

Chapter 12

It has been three days since we left the quiet of the mountains behind us. All good things must come to an end; I get it. Right about now, though, I am grateful for the callouses on every inch of my feet. Because if they were not there, blisters would be. I cannot recall the last time I had a blister, but what I do recall is how much they suck. We have been at this particular rest stop for going on approximately four hours now. How much money we have made, I am not sure. It is really not my business, so I do not even count anymore. All the people's face, their cars, and how much I have talked them out of their pockets, purses, or wallets just end up blurring together by the time we are done anyway.

Growing up like this did not seem all that strange to a kid that has never known anything else. We did not compare it to people who grow up in houses and stuff like that. Besides, Daddy said it is better than that because we get to go wherever we want, whenever we want. I could see him sitting on a lawn chair he placed by the walkway going up to the restrooms. He was holding a pair of needle nose pliers and a piece of coat hanger. We spent the entire morning digging through bee-ridden trash cans from the previous day's travelers. We picked out aluminum cans and rinsing all of them out in the spout surrounded by the bed of rocks that everyone washes random things from their cars off with, like dishes or crap on their shoe. I, sometimes, have a repeating dream of myself pulling my pants down to pee on the rocks of a faucet similar to that one, and when I wake up, I find that I have wet myself in my sleep.

All the cans we find went to a pile by Daddy and were cut in certain ways so that he could fashion them into different pieces of art that he sold as handmade crafts to interested folks passing through. I have seen him design all sorts of things, from pinwheels for gardens, outhouse scenes, and airplanes, with simple items, such as aluminum cans, shells, and beer tabs. He also burned wood with a magnifying glass he kept in the glovebox. He reminded us constantly to keep our eyes peeled for the right type of wood. Normally, he would use it to sell someone a customized work of art with their kid's name burned into it or some sentimental article of sorts. Very personal to people who would not be able to come up with ideas like that on their own. He would even show them how to do it for their little ones as a perk for buying one—fun-for-the-whole-family kind of promises. It worked well enough, I imagine.

Daddy was an exceptionally talented man, an artist of imagination and master of random creation, but mostly just a genius at manipulation. He had definitely fine-tuned the art of making something out of nothing, that is for sure.

Bubba and Hellion were walking up to the newest vehicle pulling in, as my mind wandered back from Daddy. They reached up and handed over the note that Daddy wrote earlier that morning. I did not see what he jotted on this one specifically, but I am pretty positive it reads something like this: "Hi, my family needs your help. My parents have five children and recently lost their jobs. We are very hungry, and if you could spare any kind of money to feed us until my dad can get back to work, my family would be grateful. God bless you and have a wonderful day."

Watching the driver look my little brothers up and down, I could tell he noticed the dirt on their faces, the lack of shoes on their feet, and the ragged clothes Daddy made us wear when we were working. I heard one of them crying from here, but this late in the day I could never be sure of whether it was on purpose or just because they were tired from the constant rigmarole. The monotony of the routine that came with panhandling can make you a bit insane after a while, and you can get to a point where you start feeling like you are in an episode of the *Twilight Zone* and you find yourself searching for shadows of Alfred Hitchcock to pop up on wall somewhere. It can get the best of you if you are not a seasoned veteran like Sissy and myself. With one final sweep of his eyes across the parking lot in search of these benevolent parents of theirs, I caught the driver's eyes fall upon Daddy doing his crafts, then on the Witch and Baby Girl, and it was all but a matter of time from there. No one walked away at that.

Looking down into his lap I could see him adjust his weight to reach for his wallet, rolled the window all the way down, and handed the boys their fare. I could not tell the difference in the bills, but I smiled because I knew it was just one step closer to shutting it down for the day.

I did not think Daddy ever has a set amount he is aiming for specifically, but I could be wrong. Knowing Daddy, it probably was a set amount, but only changes every time the goal he was trying to achieve has changed. One can never guess at these kinds of things, so I just brushed it off. Seeing my brothers thank the man, we all began to run toward Daddy. I liked to get excited for them. I could feel it lift their spirits, like they had done something to be really proud of, but also, I felt it gave them the energy to keep driving on, even when I knew for certain they were done an hour or more ago. The soul of a child can be easily influenced into distracting its own mind to earn the reward of a parent's love. I used to think it was a beautiful thing. That was until I realized that most parents did not use this power over their kids for good. Instead, they lied to them, manipulated them, and used them. They ignored their kids' efforts of affectionate and attention to benefit themselves or their own egos and well-being for one reason or another.

Adults have a different aura about them. A dull sense of self-awareness or detached air of value to the innocent. Maybe because of dealings with desensitization done in part by their own parents or maybe some tragedy along the way; who knows? But children have a bright, burning, fire of color and light glowing around them in every direction that is hard to separate when attempting to depict the presence of it versus their soul. I do know that the man, whose voice I hear constantly in my ear, tells me that it is a mixture

of innocence and something put in them that I have never heard anyone else mention, called the Holy Spirit of God. What that means,
I am not sure, but I listen and look for it everywhere. I cannot ask
anyone because no one else hears the man that speaks to me. I know.
I have tried to explain it before, and everyone started making fun of
me. Saying that, I had imaginary friends.

Daddy did not like that cause, I reckon; it made him look bad,
so he told me never to mention him or anyone else, for that matter,
again, or he would tan my hide. It made him look like a "bad parent," he said. I thought about saying that he had that all taken care of
himself by the way folks looked at us at the rest stops but had decided
it was best just to nod and agree.

Sissy liked to walk on the wild side of life as a child, and ever
since the darkness of Daddy's wrath had devoured her soul, she has
gone the extra mile to defy him intentionally. It has become some
sort of game with her. I cannot tell yet whether it is because she
wants to get even or if it is because she has lost her ability to give a
fuck. Either way, it is extremely dangerous, and not just to her, but
all of us. Even Daddy. He has not taken the time to notice it. It is
obvious to me that he believes that we are all still in the same phase
of innocence as the boys. Maybe he thinks children stay that way.
Maybe he just does not know yet because he does not have any kids
that are grown.

Parents are blind to the changes in kids, especially their own. A
kid only needs one moment of clarity, I call it. Or moment of truth.
When a parent shows them who they really are, and they finally,
believe it, then that determines from that instance forward whether
the word *Mom* or *Dad* is the name they continue to praise or not.

For Sissy, that had all been altered long ago. I look at her dark-
ened heart, and it breaks mine. We do not talk much anymore.
Though, when she does finally say something, I listen. All of us kids
do because we know. She is not the same and never will be again. The
car she is making a bee line for is the same familiar shape of a vehicle
known all too well by us kids as a car to avoid. Specifically because
it is considered an "unmarked" car, one the laws use, to trick us outlaws by taking all the writing and lights off it. I think it is completely

ignorant to use the exact model vehicle you use with writing, as you do without, but you cannot really explain that to a pig. Can you? I went to stop her, but she just turned and walked away. I knew she would just cause a scene and find a way to make it my fault because there is no way in hell she did not know that car was a cop. The farther I could get from the tragedy about to unfold, the better.

Then I cannot be involved, even accidentally. Honestly, I was hoping I could give her room to do something that will make Daddy want to throw all of his crafts and us along with them into the car and make a mad dash out of here. Spotting another RV roll into the parking space, two spots down from where I was standing near Daddy, I took it as my clue to get to work. As they put it in park, I was already moving in their direction. Daddy let out a low whistle, like the old Westerns that play when a tumbleweed blows by, and it told me that he wanted to handle that one. Of course, he did! That was guaranteed money in the bank with his artsy can crap.

They had room to put stuff in that mobile command center called a recreational vehicle. Asshole. That was like stealing candy from a baby, or so he likes to say. I think that anyone who would steal candy from a kid, let alone a baby, has got to be one hell of a prick. Who does that kind of stuff and brags about it out loud? I know it is just a saying, but it had to come from somewhere, right?

That was about when I saw Bud for the first time. He drove his little sky-blue Chevrette in between the line of cars parallel with the RV to the left if you were facing the building behind Daddy. I left my attitude with the roots my feet had been growing into the pavement waiting for another car to pull up, moseyed right on up to the passenger side to look as pathetic and confused as possible, then began to jerk tears into my eyes. I recall the sweat from the heat of the summer beading down my face, the sun slightly blinding me, and the way I could smell the dirt on my hands and taste the salt from my sweat in the corner of my mouth.

I remember him clearly. He was a round, old man that appeared not gentle but timid, carefree but not trusting of the people around him. His smile said one thing, and his body said another. All I kept thinking was "What is he hiding?" Off jump, he made me nervous, but when he climbed out and moved toward me, I did not miss a beat and went right into my routine.

Crouching down to get eye level with me, he flashed his smile again, then reached for my hand. I flinched as he did, and he raised his head and eyes to take in the scene around us. I knew he could not see Daddy yet because of the RV. But just because Daddy was there did not mean I was all right with him touching my hand. He was creepy, and his soul was thin and felt dark and empty. I have been around his kind before. But I knew I could make this quick. By appearances, you could see he was not a man of wealth right away. But he reached into the brown leather wallet he had stashed in his front pocket of his shorts, and he slipped out a $100 bill. Placing it in my hand, he squeezed mine shut into a fist with his wrapped around it and the other clasped on top. As he did, he looked me in the eye to ensure I understood when he stated that he was going to the restroom and wanted me to be right there when he got out. I did not have to say a thing. I just nodded like I do when Daddy asks me if I understand. Of course, I do, but you think that implies that I will listen? I may be nodding, but as he walked away, I was thinking, "Hell *no*, stupid!"

Once he was inside, still gripping the money as hard as I can, I bolted straight around that big hunk of metal that was in my way to glorious victory. The boys and I all arrived at Daddy's side at the same time with cash in hand. Sissy came skipping up with a shit-eating grin like she was about to make me look bad somehow, so I let them go first to make sure she did not do just that. They had a five and ten, and she whipped out her ten and twenty, then showed her teeth in a mock "Ha-I'm-the-best" display of arrogance. She truly just did not care anymore. She had lost her sense of self-worth and joy in the little things.

When I saw the money in his hand and his eyes light up as he went to congratulate her, I remembered the bill crinkled tightly inside my dirty fist. I did not want to give it to him. Everything inside of me said not to do that to her. The hair raising on the back of my neck, though, told me that there was no longer an option to hide it. I knew without turning that Bud was almost upon us. His soul's cloudy must crept up, long before he did, and Daddy gazed from his chair without lifting his head from his diligent work. The man strutted right up behind me like we were old friends and said, "Hey, honey. Is this your Daddy? Did you tell him what Uncle Bud gave you, precious?" Then he was so bold as to place his firm but wrinkled old-man hand upon my shoulder. At that, I did my best to shrug it off but did not beat Daddy to the punch. He was up on his feet and smacked the man's hand right off before I could even finish my shrug. Daddy did not say anything. He just stood there in a firm stance, directly in Bud's face, staring straight in his eyes, as if to say "And *what*?" without having to say anything at all.

Stammering out his words, he did his best to explain to Daddy what had transpired prior to his introduction to the head of my household. I interrupted somewhere right before he spit out that he gave me money by tugging on Daddy's shirt and holding up my opened hand to reveal the crinkled-up trophy of Bud's intentions. With one simple, silent gesture, I had shifted the entire course of the negative force that had almost reached its crescendo. The wave of relief that melted from the shell of a sickened man that was just cowering behind me versus the delighted ill-intended reckoning of the evil void standing before me. Oh, how I could taste their similarities of destruction and manipulation, crisp in my mouth. I had to lean over to spit it out, for fear that I risk contamination or infection from their darkness combined. Daddy's gleam of excitement only increased as he snatched the wad from my palm to unfold and examine it fully. At the onset of Daddy's shift in character, Bud's followed suite.

There was something wrong with this situation, and I got a flash of red, hard, and boiling hot, like fire flowing through me. These moments have been all too frequent lately for me not to recognize the fact that something in the universe has been altered and the changes in me are so significant that I dare not to imagine the future for fear that I may disrupt it unwillingly.

Chapter 13

losing my eyes, I was imagining a field on the edge of a cliff, just outside of the city. It was nighttime, and the fireworks from the Fourth of July display were bright and colorful arrays of light and energy dripping and sizzling high above the crowd. The sound of Daddy's voice brought me back to the sun shining upon my face and cracking the creases of my lips, as I stood in the dead grass of that Texas rest area. Bud and Daddy have been going at it for an hour about his stupid crafts and idealistic hopes for their future partnership. Though he was doing a great job at convincing Daddy of his interest in it all, I do not buy it for one second.

I could see Daddy's love of his own mind's creations flowing out of him and the greed of the dark cloud above. He had no idea how his exaggerations appear completely revealed to someone like me, or maybe, he did. But to the intended audience, Daddy would seem wise beyond pure genius. Cunning, as one may believe they are, they were too wrapped up in their own ego and deceit to even notice the approach of another spider on their web or spinning their own right next to them.

I have never witnessed the darkness of someone's soul breed the black right into another. That was, until now. There was some aura of sickness brewing in the loom of the old man's heart, a lust of sort familiar to my senses, and I knew I wanted nothing to do with him. Once the day decided to tilt toward the evening, I was so passed exhaustion that I had come up behind it again. The moment that I heard the words "Pack up" bellowed out of Daddy's mouth, I smashed the hustle lever into full throttle. I used to get so sick in the sun in the beginning. I am talking about being physically nauseous, puking, and all that kind of jazz. Some time ago it had dawned on me that taking a taste off one of Daddy's beers or a puff or two off a left-handed cigarette may have been great for the nerves, but it sucked something fierce after being on your feet for the entire swelter of the day. Though, this far into the game, I am well passed that whole experience, I feel it thick in my throat.

After loading up and starting up the path of pavement riddled with exit signs, I scooted up on my knees and peeked over the edge of Max, who was tucked in his spot along the shelf we call a back window. There he was, crammed into the driver's seat of the gasoline fueled cloud of blue behind us, just putting along. I was not certain if he was following us or just leaving simultaneously, so I let it be.

We made our way from there to a road that led us to a left-handed turn, which had a bait shop and convenience store all in one, sitting quietly, upon its corner to the left. As we slowed to take it, I repeated my routine from the exit of the rest stop, and my throat knotted, hard and tight, as the vision of the car bumping up the road behind came slowly into sight.

Without a doubt in my mind, I knew it was him. The man that called himself Bud sat snug inside the driver's seat with a look of delight on his face and an air of worry underneath. The fear of the unknown and the inability to trust others shone through without attempt to conceal. I was assuming it was due to him not realizing he was being watched by anyone capable of seeing it. Daddy rolled the car to a stop on the left side of the street about eight to ten feet from the stop sign to the rear and right upon the edge of the road and grass. Along came the decrepit old shell idling to a halt behind us. I watched for a moment, as not to give away the fact that his presence was detected, so that I could inform Daddy when the time was right. But the old man rolled right out of his car and waddled straight to the driver's side window.

That was when it dawned on me; these were the future endeavors they spoke of in such great length earlier today. I was slightly pissed at Daddy for not letting me in on his plans, but more so at myself for not picking up on them completely. I guess I felt like they both just got one over on me, and I did not even see it coming, which made me feel foolish and that I had failed. It was vastly important to be aware of the intentions of others, especially in our world of conning and deceit.

But it was not like I plainly just missed it. They never once said anything to one another about following each other, seeing one another later, or what they were doing later in the day. Nothing! So that gave me a little more confidence back. The day had dialed the waves of heat from crests of white washing against you to ripples of sweat clinging to your skin, but ready to drip at any moment. I recognized the area but could not quite grasp exactly where we were heading that Bud would be welcome also.

Daddy reached deep into his pants pocket and unfolded a wad of cash. He individually counted out each of us kids a dollar and told us to get our "asses out of the backseat" if we wanted something from the store. Of course, we all barreled out without hesitation. Making our way inside, Daddy led us to an isle and said, "Check this out." Looking up at the sign upon the rack, I read, "Penny Candy." Remembering the crinkled cash squeezed tightly in my fist, I did the math. My eyes went wide, and my mouth spit out the words "a hundred" in sync with all the rest. Now, I know a dollar is not much to some, but to people who are taught to appreciate the value of being able to make something out of nothing, it is the difference between *struggle* and *hustle*. I say it that way because it is easier to acquire money when you already have some, but not in the obvious ways. I am just saying, opportunity seems to look your way if you are not desperate for it, even with just a buck in your pocket. If you have not a dime to your name, it seems as though, you work twice as hard just to get the first dollar. Just a theory, I guess, but it has been rather accurate so far, so I am not going to brush it off as coincidence, that's for sure. And as we speak, that buck is worth a whole hundred pieces of mouthwatering delight tucked neatly on the display before us. We all look at one another and back at Daddy. He flashed his smirk of content, knowing he had just surprised us, and reached up on a shelf. He counted off the number of small brown paper sacks as he handed

them to each one of us. We spent a good bit of time carefully select-
ing the delicacies out of the bins before us.

Daddy and Bud bought some beer and strolled to the isle on
the opposite side of the store, while pretending they were looking for
something specific. I could hear their voices, just could not make out
the words, so I stopped trying. After dropping my last choice into the
bag, I skipped up to the front near the register and waited for a sign
that I was allowed to proceed with my purchase. The clerk waved
me forward, but I moved my eyes to the floor and shook my head
to imply that I was not coming yet. The older gentleman behind the
counter was very intuitive, with a worn look about his face and his
smile of understanding separated the wrinkles to expose the kindness
in his eyes.

Holding up his first finger, he glanced around and cleared his
throat in order to address Daddy. "Sir, your very polite and well-man-
nered daughter is ready to complete her transaction but has been
very respectful in waiting for your permission. As not to hold your
festivities up on a day such as this, may I have the honor of checking
her out at the register?" Then the cashier angled his head toward me
and winked. Daddy peeked around the corner and did a once over
on the clerk, nodded, and returned to his affairs. I giggled, stepped
to the counter, and emptied the contents onto the old wooden slab
that stood between him and I.

He was the sort of man you do not encounter often in the world
we live in today. You could see a glow not just around him, but one
in which radiated white heat that poured out of his skin and spirit
like hands raised to the heavens. An air of peace, joy, and innocence
reflected through kindness and humility. A soul like that leaves nothing to question because without a doubt, you know you are safe. I
caught myself gazing in awe as he grouped the candy five at a time.
"Five, ten, fifteen, twenty," I could hear him whisper. I laid my dollar
on the space next to his delicate hand. He looked up, all of a sud-
den, in terror, eyes wide, mouth dropped, and all I could think was
"Please, Daddy, not him. Anyone but him." I just could not form
those thoughts into words before the gentleman said, "Are you trying
to rob me? I cannot give you all these pieces! You are short six cents!"

and he began to giggle like a school kid, as a piece of saliva dripped onto his chin. Realizing quickly that the dear man was trying his best to make me smile, I obliged.

Ear to ear and doused in the purest of intent, I left myself open for him to get a glance at my heart. He nodded in content and said, "No worries, little lady, a smile like that earned you the tax on that Penny Candy. Now, you go enjoy your Fourth of July!" Then he handed me a box of sparklers to share among us kids. Before I let the door I was walking out of go, I turned back to get one more last glimpse of, what the man I am not supposed to tell anyone about refers to as, the *Holy Spirit*.

Chapter 14

Once we reached the booth in the median of the road, I knew exactly what we were doing. Daddy was taking us to a lake. I had already seen the body of water peek from behind the trees and brush several times as we ventured there. The lakes in Texas were not the kind of clear streams we were used to in California, but I knew, now, it was a place we could camp also.

He purchased a campsite for the weekend from the state park employee running the booth and was given a ticket to set in the dash, so it can be seen through the window upon inspection. We were so excited because it was a holiday weekend in Texas. We all knew that meant that there was going to be huge fireworks displays of some sort. It was a double bonus due to the fact that we had literally worked the tan right into our hides today and needed some type of recovery from the suffocating heat of midsummer in the South. I remember precisely the look on all of their faces that evening as we found the perfect little cove cutout on the shore of the Grapevine Lake. I never could get over the sadness of their unknowing smiles and twinkle of innocence. Even after all we had been through, we still found a way to muster up hope for better and value the little things. There was a tree in the middle by the water, so you could park in front of it and pull off making a fire on one side of the car and our camp on the other.

They always found a way to do it like that. Sometimes, we did not set up camp. Instead, we got to all cram into the car, while Daddy and the Witch slept on the hood of it. But we always made a fire.

Daddy was fascinated with fire. So was Max. And that meant that I was without a doubt. Bubba seemed pretty enthralled with it as well.

I could hear everyone begging to go swimming, as they flooded out and onto the lakeside shore we chose as our part-time paradise. It never mattered how long we got to stay, as long as we got to go at all. Kids like us came to that decision early on in life, as not to forget to appreciate or enjoy each gift of happiness we were so blessed to encounter. When things seemed hard, it made it easier to count the things you were grateful for than to be constantly reminded of the things that made it that much harder. Bud slid his car sideways beside us but parallel with the road we came off. His expression was of relief and exhaustion, though, the darkness of his cloud thickened with the afternoon sky. We were all informed we had permission to swim for as long as Sissy let us. She's in charge after all, like always. The way of things at a lake, especially during a holiday, was that the adults would allow us the privilege to experience it on our own. They would head into town and let us babysit each other was all that truly meant.

Bud was not a regular part of this routine and definitely not a planned member of this party of bandits. If I were honest with myself, I would say I knew he would fit right in with the lot of them. Even though Daddy's in-depth conversation at the rest stop may have permitted him to follow us to this hideaway, I was almost positive that he was not quite sure whether to include him in this evening's partying. I was also 100 percent certain that he would be told to sit in the car and wait, as they went to whatever buddy's house it was that they retrieved their supplies for the event to come. Uncle did not want the "bastard" there. He said, "He don't belong, that's obvious."

Turning toward Sissy to ask her if I could strip down and get my scrawny ass in the water before the dark took the time away with it, I just thought to myself, *Man, grownups sure are blind.* The color of his heart was enough for me to know that there was a beast brewing deep within that *simple, old man.*

Getting down to the edge of the water, I looked at the murkiness in the depths of it, and I saw nothing. My feet disappeared right before my eyes and toes squished deep into the muddy bottom below. Bubba and Hellion ran wild into the lake, splashing and hollering like banshees. They were young enough then that they never even questioned whether they were supposed to leave on underwear or not. I had learned previously from a birthday party out at the Boardwalk in Santa Cruz, California, a year or two ago, that we were to use better discretion when disrobing in public swimming areas. Daddy just about had a conniption fit when we were all butt-ass naked there at the public beach. In all of our glory, he may have been yelling, but I recognized the paternal pride underneath the deep of his bark. So though the boys were in their birthday suits today, I had Wonder Woman panties on to cover all my necessaries. Sissy had followed suit with My Little Pony panties and naked Baby Girl in tow.

Looking back in time, I had one of the best times of my life with the group of my brothers and sisters out there in that Fourth of July evening sun. It sucks because I only remember it when I start this whole story from the beginning. Other than that, the scars from this night's tragedy are way too much to put oneself through time and again. At least, that is, until you just become it. You know? Become the evil yourself. Then it just seems normal. Only reason I know that is because that is exactly what ends up happening; it did to all of us anyway. In the end, nothing bothered me—not a single act of treachery, violence, horror, or atrocity. How do people expect kids to come back from things like that? I always wonder that, but I bet if I said it out loud, I would not find a soul who could answer that for me.

Once Daddy decided to take his trip without his newfound pal, we were on our own. Bud had opted for an afternoon nap while the rest of them got the bulk of supplies on hand, out of the trunk. What that really meant was that he pretended to sleep, as he peeked through his eyelids in the front seat of his car. I crept like a gator in the water, almost eye level, to take in the scene. The fire was rearing, sleeping bags and blankets were stacked by the pile of other random items, such as towels and what-not, and Sissy was on the log with Baby Girl.

Them leaving implied that Sissy no longer got to swim. You cannot take the baby in water without the grownups, and you cannot just leave her on the blanket by the fire while we played, though, I am quite sure that no one would have even known if she had. The relief of the cool water in that Texas lake was like using the aloe vera plant juice on your sunburn after a day of being scorched by the heat of a holiday sun in the midst of the southern summer and me having to enjoy it in the background while I felt Sissy's soul crying softly on the banks was almost more than I could bear the burden of facing inside my dreams that night. So I crept quietly up from the solace of that water hole and walked over to exchange that enjoyment for hers.

There is nothing in this world that I have found, so far any-way, that can change the light that burns around another human being faster than sacrificing your own happiness for theirs. Later on, throughout life, I figured out how to use that insight to heal my own torment. Days like these create memories that you want to be branded in your mind forever. Though, tonight's events are stains of pain that bleed out the valley of tears and shrieks from which wake you from nightmares that you can only pray fade away some day.

Smiling is a gift that Sissy rarely shared with the rest of the world those days, and to see one on her face almost brought tears into my eyes, as I dug around the bags Daddy left us for a towel to dry off with. About that time, Bud's jolly darkness crept up the base of my spine and into the pit of my stomach. Snapping around quickly, I realized that he was still standing about ten feet away and grinned as he asked if I need a towel. Nodding my head in the shade of the tree, as he glanced me over, I shivered slightly and crossed my arms over my chest. I knew something was off about him from the first moment, and when I think back, I already knew what was off but chose to go against my gut anyway.

He opened the front passenger door and instructed me to sit down in the seat to keep warm while he found the towel in the back of the hatch. Innocent enough, I supposed. When he came around to bring it to me, he sat in the driver's seat and closed his door, instead of just coming back to mine to hand it off. He was slick and sneaky and up to something, that I could tell, but it was apparent that he had done whatever it was he was warming up to before just by the provisions he was making to avoid my escape. That was when I decided I had had enough of my analyzing to know something was about to go down that I did not want to be involved in, and I took it upon myself to get out of his car. Before I had the chance to even turn completely to get up, he had leaned over and closed the door, then locked it. I could see Baby Girl on the blanket by the fire and Sissy and the boys in the lake, then thought to myself about the irony of it all. What a whooping I would get if Daddy came pulling back up this very moment. And I do not even want to imagine the horror Sissy would suffer!

Bud did not hesitate to brush his hand across my lap and touch my panties, as he pulled it back from the lock. As dry as they were now from that Texas heat, I wondered what made me even want a towel to begin with, especially considering how I never got one anyway. I looked downward at the feeling that he left with the trace of his fingers and then upward at his crooked smile to hear him say how much he liked my Wonder Woman panties. My stomach was in my throat already, and I choked on the words attempting to leave my dried lips. He did not miss a beat, though, and backed it up with whispering that he'd give a dollar for some more of that Penny Candy, to take them off. "I just want to get out, sir" was all I could murmur.

He sat up, looked right into my eyes, and said, "You can't! Your Daddy said you were in trouble, and you have to sit here until he gets back." I felt the heat rise into my face as I fought back the tears. I was not about to cry because of the position I was in; I was scared of what I had done to piss off Daddy. But with that thought, I felt the hate of Sissy's anger, strong and burning red, rise up over me like the fury of a California wildfire, and then heard her ask, "What are you doing, Daughter?" Before I could answer, Bud, in all his confidence that he had found the one thing that would cripple us all, repeated the statement about me being in trouble. Sissy's beat did not skip, either. She reached her hand through the window, unlocked the door, and yanked my ass up out of that seat.

Then she stared Bud dead in his eyes and poured liquid fire and ice right out of her and into the words that shut him down, no questions asked. "NO ONE PUNISHES US BUT DADDY!"

Chapter 16

Daddy and the rest of the don't-let-this-happen-to-you crew reappeared right after dark. They got settled in and unpacked everything while the fresh hamburgers were grilling. I could see Max sniffing the air, just looking for the meat. Daddy did not feed any of the animals we ever owned raw meat. He said that it would make them turn on us, and Max already knew there was a burger on the fire for him, so he just sat and wait.

Once the cooking was over and we were all eating, I began thinking about today. I looked at Daddy in shame because I had just added a secret to the pile, which seemed as if it was a mountain already. I glanced around the campfire for Sissy to give her an unsaid thanks, but when I did, she was not there. I turned my back to the heat of the flames to check on where she had run off to. I found her on the opposite side of the car near the rear driver side door in whispered conversation with the Witch. The Witch snapped her head up quickly, as if she had felt my stare. Then she pointed her index finger straight at me and signaled me to "Come here" with the end of it. Panic overcame me, instantly, and I could feel myself start to tremble, slightly. I put my paper plate on the log next to where I sat and started over to her.

When I arrived, she looked pissed. I could feel the heat from her anger over the fire from the camp, and I knew Sissy had told. The Witch stared a hole right into my eyes and said, "Is it true? Is what your sister said true?" My head turned to Sissy and then to the ground beneath my feet, which felt as if it was going to come out from under me at any moment. Sissy smacked the top of my arm with the back of her hand, as if to say "Tell her, stupid!" And I gulped out the words "Is what true?" She cleared her throat.

"What Sissy told me about Bud! And tell me *exactly* what happened, so I know you guys are telling me the truth!" I knew what that meant; she was going to tell Daddy. Sissy said softly, "It's okay, Daughter," and I looked up from the ground while tears of fear began to fall, to see Sissy's love for me pouring white light around her. She reached down for my hand, and we walked through the day's events in detail for her.

When I was done, the Witch did something I never expected. She crouched down eye-level with me and kissed my forehead. When she leaned back, she smiled and said, "Thank you for telling me the truth! I know it was hard, but I am proud of you!" Then she stood and disappeared around the other side of the car. Sissy pulled me close in a half-hug, then instructed me to just stand by her. I had never felt so safe in the midst of so much fear. When the Witch came back around the car with Daddy, all that safety fell through the floor of the earth below me. I felt like I was suspended over a never-ending pit of darkness and would fall into it and be swallowed up before anyone could save me. But then Daddy did something unexpected as well; he did not yell at me. Instead, quietly he asked me to repeat the same story and waited patiently for me to finish. The moment I was done, he turned to her and waited for her to confirm that my explanation was the same as the one I had given her. She stated firmly, "That's *exactly* what they both told me!"

Daddy nodded at her, turned back to me, and said, "It's okay, Daughter. Now, *don't repeat that to anyone again!*" Then he walked away. I felt confused, for sure. Sissy patted me in reassurance and told me to go finish my food. So I did as I was told. It was getting darker by the minute and I could feel a certain uneasiness in the air around me, but I was still so shaken by the talk that I could not separate the beads of emotion from others and mine. I knew that they would be up for hours, so I was planning on sneaking into a tent for some much-needed sleep, but when I rounded the car to crawl into one, they were gone.

Everything was! I mean *everything*! Was I drifted off in thought so long, I completely wasted away the entire night? I hope not because I knew there was not going to be much of a break on this coming day, seeing as how it was the day after the Fourth of July and *all* the travelers would be frequenting rest areas. I raised my head to the sky to seek out the moon and found it right where it was supposed to have been for about half-past midnight. That was when I knew something was wrong. Right about the time of my revelation, Sissy came up behind me and whispered for me to make sure I had everything I wanted to bring with us because we were about to leave. I nodded to her as we made our way back to the campfire. At the same time, I heard some men begin to argue. Then the Witch opened the back passenger door and beckoned for all of us kids to *load up*. She was standing in the open front passenger door in a T-shirt and tight blue jeans with no shoes on her feet. Her long blond hair was glistening brightly in the glow of the flames, and time began to stand still. I was suspended there in the space between past and future that adults call *the present*. But it was shifting into the future and becoming the past so slowly that I could feel every beat of it. Daddy bellowed out, "Are you calling my daughter a liar?" as Bud shuffled rapidly to his car and climbed behind the wheel. Uncle was already at his passenger door with it open and Daddy at the door next to Bud. I never saw it coming, and I was in slow motion. So I know Bud never saw it either. Daddy pulled something long, hard, and wooden from behind his back and struck Bud in the side of the face with it. It impacted him so hard that it knocked his entire body across the car to Uncle who, in turn, proceeded to take his steel-toed boot and field-goal kicked him right back over to Daddy. They continued the movements in what appeared to be a symbiotic rhythm of sorts. Max did a ritualistic dance of instigation around the fire and nipped every so often at the front of the car. The Witch stood cheering them on as she watched for local campers that may have been coming up the road.

Fire was barreling higher and higher with the fuel of hate that was feeding it. I could not make out Daddy's or Uncle's faces from the shadows of Bud's blood soaked across them. The darkness of that evil old man had puttered out many minutes before they ever had the thought to stop. Daddy's rage did not end when they stopped the beating of his lifeless body and left him slumped in the front seat of that wretched blue hatchback. He backed up from the car and made eye contact with the Witch, who was standing over nine feet away and also splattered with the lifeblood of the sickness Daddy had just snuffed out. He gave her the go-ahead to finish gathering the proof of our existence at the lake that night. My heart was racing, and my mind was soaking up the scene before me. Daddy took his beater, which was a broken axe handle, and smashed out every single light and window in that vehicle as Uncle searched the whole inside of it and Bud's pockets for anything of value. I had completely forgotten about the rest of us kids because not one sound came from any of them. I turned to find them levitating in that same space in time, and I knew that this was the shift of the universe that I felt when Daddy met Bud.

Chapter 17

It was not the brutality of love that night that was bothering me. It was the fact that I was glad that it happened that way, and the Witch, well, she had earned her title of *Mom* to me that gruesome night. I could feel the presence of the man that Daddy had said no one was supposed to know I could see and hear him telling me repeatedly that there was no need to worry because, no matter how bad it got; it was always going to be okay. That was when he decided to share with me his name. He called himself Jesus. And from that point on in life, he was never too far away that I could not still, at least, feel him next to me.

Repeatedly, the blood would splash the back of my eyes as I dreamt of that night. Somewhere inside the state of Arizona, I heard the sound of the sirens before I ever got a glimpse of a cop car when I sat up from my nightmare. I am not sure how long it had been since we fled the state of Texas, but it could not have been more than a day or two. Daddy's shadow games were like an art form he had invented and perfected long before my birth. It looked as though we were in the clear, though, because he drifted right passed us. I could feel the relief flow from Daddy into the remaining portion of the car and off the rest of the adults as well. That was until the second cop caught up next to the first, and the two behind them pulled alongside of us, and another two crept up on our rear.

Daddy remained fairly calm, as we were escorted kindly to the shoulder of the highway and instructed via loudspeaker to pull the vehicle over, considering the circumstances. He announced clearly to remember the rules, and we do not know anyone named Bud, nor were we at any lake. Easy enough for the lot of his hooligan kids. That is about where, I would say, my perception on life had begun to line up with the thought that people were not ever going to be what they needed to be. After a rigorous display of authority by the state and local police during the apprehension of the armed and extremely dangerous family of outlaws, as described in the National APB, the city law, that had arrived to escort the children in that endeavor, decided to take it upon themselves to let us out of the vehicle. Max had absolutely no intentions, though, of letting that happen. Uncle tried to warn them, but that was an attempt that fell on deaf ears because when we refused to come out, the crew cut cop came in to get us.

I could hear every adult screaming through the closed windows of their individual police cars and Uncle kicking the glass of his with the same bloody boots. It was just not enough to keep Max from locking his jaw onto that officer's wrist and hand as he reached for the carrier that contained Baby Girl. That officer jerked his whole arm and body at the same time as Max lunged, and they both went rolling out of the back and onto the ground. It appeared as if a rabid dog was attacking an innocent law enforcement agent.

One of the cops was smart enough to let Uncle out of the back to have him "heel" Max. Unfortunately, the officer closest was not the type to hesitate before drawing his weapon down on Max and using his trigger-happy finger. The shot rang out like some kind of explosion from a homemade bomb Daddy had showed us how to make last year. But they were louder and left a ringing in my head that I could not seem to shake out. Same ringing, almost, as having a Black Cat explode when someone throws it at you, and it gets stuck in your hair while exploding. Time began to suspend again, and I could feel the spiral from the blackhole that opened beneath me sucking me in. We all watched in horror as Max twitched with his last breath, and every officer, except the one bleeding and the one who fired the fatal blow, attempted to restrain Uncle, who just wanted to hold his *good little boy*, as he faded away before us.

After the scene on the shoulder subsided and the laws gained control of the suspects and their wretched children, who followed suite in a desperate display of violence, in way of kicking and biting like rabid animals, the cars disappeared one after another. The tears, from that afternoon, dug lines in the faces of us all that no one, not even time, could wash away. I can still look into a mirror and see them today. At the station, they gathered statements from the adults and did not even attempt to ask any of the kids a single question. I figured that, after what they did to Max in front of us, they knew it would be futile. They did, however, book Daddy and Uncle into the local jail and escort us to a foster facility abruptly, leaving Mom and Baby Girl as the only ones free to walk out.

Two weeks into eating the same grapefruit breakfast and sleeping in a crammed room full of bunks, like sailors on a submarine minus the grapefruit, we got a visit from Mom. She sat me down and explained that Daddy had instructed her to tell me to talk to the detective that was going to pay me a visit later. Then she gave me the code word, so I knew the message was from Daddy. Each time Daddy got out of something, he would issue us kids a new word and not tell her or anyone for that matter, so we knew what to do in case of an emergency. It allowed us to receive instructions that we would actually follow because people always knew that a kid would listen if they felt that they were told to do so by a parent. When she had first told me to tell the truth, I thought she was full of crap because of Daddy's previous demands on that Arizona highway and all the implications that led to a conviction, but the code word was what let me know it was safe to tell the detective.

The detective from the criminal investigation division, out of the county Daddy was currently housed in, arrived right on schedule. I had nowhere else I was allowed to be, so I was there waiting ever so patiently. After explaining in tragic detail, including the tears, which were not fake this time, I saw a look of sympathy wash across his face, and I knew it was something that made sense to him. Waking the next morning to another damn grapefruit made me sick, so I left it on the plate next to the runny, scrambled eggs and went back to my bunk to clear my head. Moments later, the robust woman who ran the home and always smelled like she was the one who also picked the grapefruits, opened the door and informed us that our parent was on her way. Normally, we would have all smarted off about her *not* being our parent, but not today. I realized at that moment that we were all in agreeance; she was all of *our* mom.

We did not come there with anything but the clothes on our backs and wanted to leave the same way, so we just put on our shoes and walked to the front like she instructed us to do once we were through. Standing there with crooked grins and crazy eyes was my entire family. My heart could not bear one more unexpected turn of events, but this one was the one it could if it had to. And right now, it needed this surprise.

On the way to Bakersfield, we dropped Uncle off at one of his buddies' houses. He told Daddy that he was going to sit the next round out. I think that losing Max took the life right out of him. We said our farewells and hit the highway once again. This time Daddy did not even think about pulling over at a rest stop, not even to use the bathroom. The whole time, going to pee never even crossed my mind. All I could do was listen intently as Daddy went on to regale the tale of how they had not killed Bud after all. Bud had woken from being knocked unconscious from the first blow and dragged himself to another campsite, where he had proclaimed that a band of thieves had violently beaten and robbed him while he was camping alone. Since his ticket from the park stated "One camper and one vehicle only," it seemed believable. The local ambulance had rushed him to the emergency room, where he then made the report with the authorities. Everything he told them was a lie, though, even his real name.

The police in Texas had done their investigation thoroughly and with someone who knew their job because the report stated that the crime scene was too suspicious. The lakeside scene portrayed retribution and vengeance, due to the acts of violence and amount of damage that was done to the victim's vehicle, only after the beating and robbery had occurred. Why would someone remain at scene of a crime to possibly get caught in the act of smashing out all the windows and headlights and totaling the entire vehicle with an axe handle unless it was personal. So the police decided to run the victim's information in order to check out his character, and once it was found to be felonious, they began to look into it further. Daddy knew then that he was good to go, so he said that he wanted them to speak with me, and after the detective's report was reviewed, Bud mysteriously disappeared from his hospital room.

Daddy and Uncle were released from jail with a future request from the authorities to call them first next time. Daddy scoffed at their attempt, but once he was informed that he could just chain them to the bumper and drag them to the station, he smiled and agreed that he might be able to fulfill that request.

Chapter 18

The name of the cheap motel was something close enough to the Holiday Inn that it would trick you if you used just a phone-book to purchase a room, especially if you did not know the difference in a hotel and a motel. Good thing we were never trying to get a room at a fancy hotel. Daddy said those sorts of joints required too much information for his liking and were "busy bod-ies." What he probably meant was that the maid came into the room against your request and that you had to have identification to rent it in the first place. Daddy did not believe in having any form of identification for anyone, except us, because he used it to get his government assistance in each state we would frequent.

There was a fenced-in pool in the middle of the drive, and the parking lot circled the whole swimming area in the shape of a horse-shoe. Each space lined up to the doorway of the room and had the number for that room stenciled onto the space and the curb in front of it. I am assuming because of the conflicts people create over a single parking spot because it was not like the door was not close enough to match the number to the key with the big plastic ring that had the room number printed directly on it. The only real issue was reading the key ring because it was normally worn so hard from the constant use that you had to make sure that your receipt matched instead.

The train tracks that led into downtown, or at least close enough to walk the rest of the way, were across the main drag by the motel. The local train came on time every day, except the first day we jumped it, but only because we were guessing at the time then. The empty rail car doors were always left wide open, and the whole train moved so slow that they could boost most of us on while the train was moving, and Sissy and I jumped up the ladder and climbed aboard. The day after we got the room, we took the train as close as we could, stepped off the ladder on the side, and walked the remaining few miles to the Department of Social Services. Mom had to apply for Daddy's well-earned checks and food stamps. Back then, food stamps were just that, stamps, and the checks were checks.

While Mom took us to do that, Daddy went and found a job working for the pizza place around the corner from the room, as a cook. What that told me was that we were planning on being here for a little while, and that meant we would get a break. I guess he knew we needed one. Maybe not. Maybe he just needed one, and it so happened to work out for everyone. I do not care. Either way worked for me.

The days were turning fast, and we moved from one room to the next, but always at the same motel. Besides the male housekeeper, no one else tried anything with me, but I was not about to tell Daddy about that because I did not want to have to go back to foster care. I hate grapefruit. Besides, I got out of it unscathed, so I was not concerned. It just taught me how to pay more attention to the intentions of men. Mom spent her nights walking the blade with the rest of the prostitutes while Daddy ran with the boys or worked at the parlor. We ate so much pizza, you would think that I would have never wanted to see another one by the time we were older, but for some reason or another, it is still one of my favorite foods. When Mom would land a john, she would have them wait outside for a second so she could come tell us to hide in the bathroom and play the quiet game. When they would give her the money, she would throw the bills into the bathroom and let us hold them until she was through. My belief is that it was her way of distracting us as we listened to the act of consummation taking place through the door. I remember one night, Daddy had come home upset while she was still out on the track, and shortly after, she had come back explaining about the officer who finger-banged her right there on the strip so she could avoid a night in the slammer.

He wanted to sue the police department. She told him, "Stop being ridiculous, because in all actuality, we would not win that fight." He had finally listened to reason but told her to take a break for about a week to let everything cool down. Halloween came up fast, and Daddy had decided that in place of buying costumes, he would paint all of our faces like clowns. The only paint he had handy was the car modeling paint from the model kits he had taken up as his most recent artistic hobby. So he painted all of our faces with it, including Baby Girl's. It was awesome! We were the coolest costumes out that night and came back with pillowcases full of candy.

The only problem was getting it off your face without the turpentine. The rashes it left peeling off and rubbing so hard with the washcloth the next morning were worth every bit of it to kids like us. Better than the ass-whooping we would have gotten if we cried while taking it off.

Before long, I got to finally take that trip to see Mama. When we came back and Daddy found her number, it was all over. I was mad at myself. Not just because she had played me, but because I ruined it for the rest of the family. We had had a great life there, and I took that from all of us. I had even stolen the love between Daddy and Mom, and it was a hurt I wished every moment after that I could scrub off, just like the paint on my face from that last Halloween.

Once Daddy's revolver was found in the glove box, it was strictly standard procedure from there. They cuffed Daddy, and all us kids began to cry so loud the group of uniforms outside the car turned in our direction. It was apparent that they can hear us, but none of them even budged. Daddy noticed their response and requested that the arresting officer allow him to say his goodbyes to his children, crying in the backseat.

The man grabbed the center links that locked his hands to one another and dragged him in an awkward manner toward the back door. Shuffling, in sync, behind the man with the badge, Daddy appeared smaller than normal. When the gentleman reached for the handle, that was all the permission we required.

Pouring out of the metal entrapment containing every last memory I had of him, we sniffled and sobbed openly and without fear of punishment or judgment. By the look that fell upon the officer, he did not intend on letting us out or allowing us to hug or touch him when he brought him to us. I guess he imagined four hysterical children were going to sit there on the cold, hard leather and watch through the open space between as their hero, father, protector, teacher, and God said a few encouraging words and waved their lives and futures into oblivion and chaos.

Instead of forcing us back into the car, the cop surprisingly released his grip on the restraints, which contained what he once believed to be a violent and treacherous crime suspect and threat to the community in which he served. It encouraged the lot of us, hooligans, to adorn our now loving father kneeling before us in tears of humility and grief.

On any other occasion, I would have smiled behind my tear-filled lying eyes, and I would have watched in awe as Daddy pulled off his award-winning performance with such finesse, but today was not that "any other occasion." He had an air of confidence about him always. He goes ever so peaceful and cooperative on all of our normal, illegal encounters. So to the others, it may seem as if everything is going to be all right. By the way he went along with the situation so comfortably, no one would ever have suspected him of guilt.

Mannerisms alone suggested otherwise, regardless of the facts stacked obviously against him. Not a single care in the world or a whisper of anything but silence, decked head to toe with inked memories promoted by his faded-out tattoos. The ranking officer separated himself from the crowd of others, walked up to Daddy, and excused him for the long haul. Crawling back into the heated space inside of our cage, I watched through the back glass window where Max, Uncle's dog, used to lie before the last event's officers shot him on that Arizona highway for protecting us kids. I wished he were here to help Daddy right now, but facts is he was not.

Dragging him toward his own empty police interceptor, Daddy looked back one final time and lifted one hand, as far around as he could, for us to witness him signing "I love you" with his index finger, thumb, and pinkie. His tears were flowing down his cheeks for all the onlooking pedestrians and that morning's job-goers to see.

I would like to say that was when I realized that it was everything I feared. He was not coming back, not this time. But I knew it was the end the moment he requested to say his farewells. You see, Daddy never had to tell us bye because he always knew he was going to be coming home shortly after. For him, it was "Till next time" always. Well, except now. By the time the wrecker towed the "suspect's vehicle" away, the officers had already contacted the local women and children's shelter in that farewell county for available beds.

One agreed to escort us over to claim ours in his unmarked car that arrived only moments after they hauled my father out of my life forever. The shelter provided what was left of my family, with a single room containing two sets of bunk beds, one on each side of the room. The walls were unadorned, plain, white, and vacant of a sense of home. We all were able to remain in the same room, though, which made it a little less hollow.

Days fade into weeks, and word came that Daddy was staring down the barrel of a large stent in the penitentiary without mention of just how long that sentence for strong armed robbery would truly end up being. I close my eyes and can still recall the streaks of pain rolling down his face, on all of ours, and I remember the love and pain we shared through all of our tragedies and struggles.

Chapter 20

When it comes down to it, I am just that little girl. The one who looked up, saw the word *Daddy* standing before me, and was amazed. The one who just wanted to have someone love me as much as I loved the world and everything in it. The one who did not understand why people were so hurtful and intentionally evil. The one who found herself not knowing why anyone could ever think that she could or would be anything like the rest of them. The one who, despite how many times her heart was broken, dreams or hopes were shattered, or was left abandoned by the entire world, did not become just like anyone or anything. I had just become *nothing*.

I knew what Daddy was then, and I know what Daddy is now. I no longer desire to be what Daddy was or has become. There I stood, an empty shell they called *outlaw*. Sick to my stomach, I asked God and myself, "Who in their right mind would choose the depths of hell over every wonderful thing they have ever experienced, just to save the ones who do their best to make this world what it has become? Who would become what they hated the most just to prove to them all that there was a way? A way to love them. A way to forgive them. A way to understand or accept them for who they were or what they have done. A way to love and forgive herself for ever believing that it was her fault or that she made them that way. A way to overcome the obstacles of her environment. A way to break free from the chains in which she had become enslaved." I would! I have! And I will continue to do the same. Because I have found a way. A way to interact with the rest of the world and still be what I was created to be. A leader. A soldier in a different army. A warrior for a new kind of battle. The one being waged in the unseen realm. An outlaw for a *new world order*.

The end of days is upon us. Every day, I can see the way it changes. The entities of the unknown dimensions are gathering. They are restless and eager for war. The God of us all is coming to separate his chosen and judge the remaining for what they have done. "Each morning brings a renewed spirit," that is what it says. That is because we are going to need to be recharged for each day's untold tragedy created by the monsters of the society around us, intending, only to destroy any good that may remain. By nightfall, the void of the darkness will swallow you whole if you do not allow God's spirit to rejuvenate you. Its temptress will cry out to your flesh and entice your heart's evil desires. I know. I have been through it all. I have been all of you, walked in all of your shoes, tasted all of your pleasures, and indulged in all of your pain. Inside and out. I now understand why. You cannot share the experience of God on a significantly altering personal level if you cannot empathize with the ones that the message is intended to reach.

He did not send me for those of them who believe that they do *not* need a savior. He is coming back for us—the ones who do not know that there is one but whose souls plead for that Savior daily and the ones that are or have been abandoned to the darkness by the bulk of society, and who do what we know how to do best? *We survive!* These lost and broken soldiers of the streets are my brothers and sisters, not in marriage or blood, but in *suffering and sin*!

And I am his daughter, *Daughter Outlaw*!

To be continued...